Angels or ALIENS?

JAMES BROUILLETTE

ISBN 978-1-64569-886-9 (paperback)
ISBN 978-1-64569-887-6 (digital)

Christian Faith Publishing, Inc.
832 Park Avenue
Meadville, PA 16335
www.christianfaithpublishing.com

Printed in the United States of America

Contents

Introduction

At the age of 21, although I didn't know it at the time, I read a book that changed my life. I had been educated for twelve years in parochial school, and I was then dumped into the California State University system. There, I was duly indoctrinated by a largely secular faculty that challenged every Christian belief I had been taught. I had already begun to question many of the doctrines of the denomination in which I was raised by the time I got to college. The first doctrinal cracks began around the age of thirteen, when overnight it was no longer a Mortal Sin to eat meat on Fridays, so I was primed to be a disbeliever by the time I turned twenty-one. From the discrepancies I learned about Christmas and Easter, to an inability to defend the Virgin Birth, I was red meat for many of my professors at Long Beach State University. I bet that's difficult for some millennials to imagine! In this day of artificial insemination and even gene manipulation, a pregnancy happening without having sex is more than physically possible, it is now an everyday occurrence. Yet back then, a virgin birth was a deal breaker for me.

Eric von Daniken's book *Chariots of the Gods* was translated into English in 1969, the same year we landed on the moon. Von Daniken states that he attended boarding school and was taught by the Jesuits. During his three years with the Jesuits, von Daniken says he and his classmates translated the Bible from language to language. I read his book shortly after it came out in paperback, and it had a profound effect on me. Von Daniken says that he first began questioning some biblical accounts when, in the first book of Moses, God descends to the mountain and there is rumbling and smoke and fire. Von Daniken says he thought to himself, "This is not my God... My God does not need a vehicle to travel around in." At the time his statement seemed reasonable, but now after years of reflection, I have no idea how he reached this conclusion. I will discuss why God needs a vehicle to travel between dimensions later in detail.

Throughout the following years the ideas in *Chariots of the Gods*, and von Daniken's next book, *Gods from Outer Space*, sat in the back of my mind like a pulsing, burning chunk of coal. The books presented astounding evidence, and I thought von Daniken's theories might have some validity. Remains of batteries found in the ruins of Bronze Age cities, cave drawings of alien looking people, and amazing gigantic stones cut to fit with laser-perfect precision filled his books. It was like chocolate ice cream with peanut sprinkles for my imagination, and of course, at the time, I was very impressionable. But at the same time I was impressionable, I had also developed some pretty good tools for logical thinking, and all this new amazing information seemed to make sense. I embraced many of the ideas presented in *Chariots of the Gods*. I wasn't looking for a new religion; I was on a crusade to discover some personal truths, and it seemed to me at the time, I was on the right path.

Von Daniken once stated that he was steered toward the book of Enoch by the Jesuits. It was in this book he says that he first read Enoch was taken up in a fiery chariot. Von Daniken then found the book of Ezekiel, where in my opinion, chapters 1 and 10 contains excellent descriptions of the vehicle that brought God to earth along with his throne. Von Daniken also states that the book of Enoch talks about the Fallen Angels that came down to earth from heaven and had intercourse with women (daughters of Adam) and had offspring who were giants. While the book of Enoch is a non-canonized book of the Bible, you can also find this same account in the book of Genesis; chapter 6 verses 1 through 5 of the King James Version of the Bible. In fact, according to Genesis, it was this abomination that caused God to bring on the flood of Noah.

Eric von Daniken recently stated he is not out to start a new religion either. In fact, he says, he would turn over in his grave if a religion based on his findings was ever formed. I'm sure some would disagree, but while challenging many of the beliefs of modern-day Christianity, along with those of most other mainstream religions, the whole ANCIENT ASTRONAUT (ALIEN) view in many ways seems like a new religion. The followers of von Daniken's original theories, who I will call ANCIENT ASTRONAUT THEORIESTS, show many traits like those of the followers of mainstream religion. Most of these ANCIENT ASTRONAUT THEORIESTS suffer the same type of shunning, by the "scientific experts," von Daniken has suffered over the years. These "fringe scientists" have been written off as unlearned and unprofessional by mainstream science. As much as they may try, however, mainstream science has not been able to discredit, or even reasonably explain many of the discoveries of this group known as ANCIENT ASTRONAUT THEORIESTS.

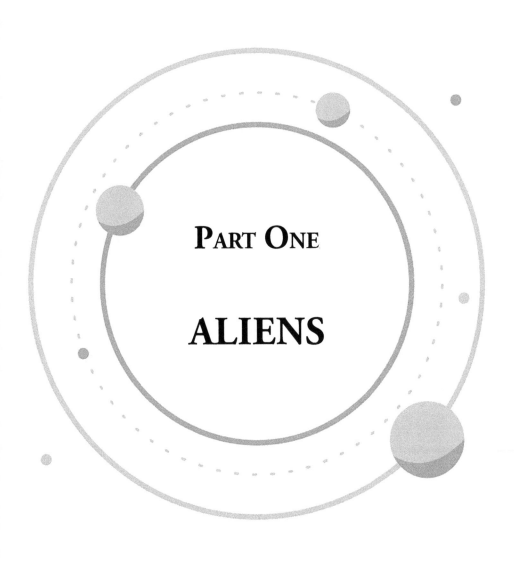

PART ONE

ALIENS

CHAPTER 1

Alien Mania

Currently, we are increasingly being bombarded from several different directions, with the idea that extraterrestrial life on other planets will soon be discovered. The idea has been around for a very long time, I can remember a show called SPACE PATROL from my youth in the 1950s, when I was five or six years old. The program was about a crew of "astronauts" in the future who traveled around from galaxy to galaxy discovering new and exciting planets that were teaming with different types of life and numerous types of villainous extraterrestrials. Our culture has embraced the sci-fi community with open arms. Some of the biggest box office hits in American movie-making history have been about space exploration, and its results. From *Star Trek* to *Star Wars*, and from 2001 *Space Odyssey* to *The Terminator* we have been given a view of the universe that includes extraterrestrial aliens, free-thinking robots, and the development of artificial intelligence, all of which is not only mind-bogglingly prophetic, but frightening as well. From the 1950s and '60s until today, we have received a continuous stream of books, movies, and TV shows that present extraterrestrial life as an absolute certainty. Now, there is at least one entire TV cable channel devoted to science fiction, and that's only if you don't count any of the cable news channels. Whether it is the *X-Files* or *Men in Black*, the theme is the same: we are not alone. Do you remember the movie *Contact*? Much of the ongoing search for extraterrestrial life, somewhere out in the universe, began with or at least was juggernauted by that book and movie. If you think about it, we have had the idea of a man who could fly that was from a planet called Krypton, for over eighty years.

We begin lying to our children early in the United States. Along with the myths of Santa Claus, the Tooth Fairy, and the Easter Bunny, we also provide them with cartoon after cartoon, animated feature after animated feature that build an allusion of reality that is false. I'm not just talking about the crazy old cartoons about a road runner and a coyote, or a cat named Tom and a mouse named Jerry; I'm talking about a multitude of animated pieces that show the future as being ultra-high-tech and often include extraterrestrial beings. Sci-fi cartoons and animations are so numerous that Wikipedia doesn't even offer a list of them. I'm sure you can think of several, in the beginning there was Flash Gordon and Buck Rogers and then later the Jetsons, and by now almost every sci-fi comic book superhero ever created has been turned into an animated feature.

Eventually parents, or someone, will tell the children the truth about Santa Claus, the Tooth Fairy, and the Easter Bunny, but who tells them the truth about aliens from outer space? The problem is, a large percent of the adult population believes this lie too. From an early age, our children are predisposed to accept the idea of space travel, interaction with space aliens, and even the idea of interbreeding between humans and extraterrestrial beings. Didn't Superman and Lois Lane have a child? Again, the subliminal indoctrination is astounding.

I remember hearing, as far back as I can remember that there are so many planets and galaxies in the universe that it is inconceivable that some of them do not support life forms of many different types. The possibility of humans here on earth being the only intelligent life in the entire universe has been deemed by academia as implausible, ridiculous, and impossible. Our children are taught in school that it is only a matter of time until we find life on another planet. Telescopes search the stars continuously for some sign of life to support their theories. We've scratched the surfaces of the Moon and Mars searching for some type of life, inferring the nonlogical conclusion that if we find life there intelligent life must exist in outer space too. Scientists all over the world listen for radio transmissions coming from deep space. Now, even though they have pursued this practice for decades, without hearing a single unexplainable beep, they continue daily expecting to find the Holy Grail at any time.

As it turns out, however, over the years we've found that some of the reasoning used for the conclusion that the discovery of life on other planets is inevitable, is majorly flawed. I remember when I was in high school before we ever stepped foot on the moon, I was taught the necessary components for life on a planet were only twofold.

Scientists like Carl Sagan told us that there were only two conditions that needed to be fulfilled for a planet to support life. It was the belief that (1) certain types of stars were necessary, and (2) there needed to be a planet just the right distance from those stars. Using these two requirements, there would be an enormous number of stars in the universe that could have a planet that would be able to support life. Because of the large number of planets, stars, and galaxies in the universe, it was concluded; there would be a huge number of planets that would be able to support life. In chapter 4 of his book *Miracles*, Eric Metaxas puts things into focus when he reports the number of possible planets capable of supporting life was shrinking. Metaxas says the number of variables necessary for life to exist on a planet in the universe has grown tremendously, while the number of planets capable of supporting life has shrunk to a number way below zero. Metaxas goes on to say that the odds are so bad it is extremely improbable that there are any planets in the universe that support life, in fact he says statistically it should be impossible that life exists on earth.

In the fourth chapter of his book, Metaxas lists item after item that is necessary for life to exist, and yet so unlikely is their existence here on earth that he believes it is a miracle that we are here. He points out that by 2001, the number of specific characteristics necessary for life had grown to 150, and that the odds against a planet supporting life was more than one in ten to the seventy-third-power. If you were to write that number, it would be a 1 followed by seventy-three zeros.

The movies we watch, show men and women exploring other planets in spacesuits that protect them from the violent atmospheres of the various planets that they will visit. The landing on the moon sealed the deal. Here were mortal humans dressed in those futuristic spacesuits, walking on the moon. However, the seldom discussed truth discovered on that moon landing was that the atmosphere on the moon would create a very difficult problem for any colonization attempt. Have you ever wondered why we haven't gone back? Science fiction meets reality.

As science makes more discoveries about the development of life and begins to discover more of the amazing requirements for life to exist on other planets, the number of things necessary for life to exist here on earth becomes larger and larger. Things that we never think about are so important; items or conditions if missing would prevent life from existing on this planet. As an example, the exact distance the Earth is from the Moon allows life as we know it to exist on this planet. If there was only a slight variance in that distance, tides would be so high, human life would be impossible.

The alien mania that has gripped our culture is so widespread you can find it almost anywhere you look. As an example, I recently searched the phrase "aliens on earth" through Google and the search produced 76,500,000 results. Here are three of the astounding headlines that jumped out at me:

> *"At least four known alien species have been visiting Earth..."*
> *"Five alien species in contact with Earth right now..."*
> *"Aliens on earth have been around for a long time..."*

The list continues on and on. Some of the hot topics on the internet concerning aliens and earth are star gates, wormholes, robots, transformers, artificial intelligence gone wild, and government confirmation of alien existence. NASA recently threw gasoline on this already hot topic by announcing a new position at the agency, and some feel that by their recent actions NASA is confirming the existence of extraterrestrial life. NASA is publicly advertising for the position of "Planetary Protection Officer." What this position at NASA entails is still up for debate, but you can be sure that many believe the main duties of this job will be to liaison between extraterrestrials and the government. According to NASA, "planetary protection reflects both the unknown nature of the space environment and the desire of the scientific community to preserve the pristine nature of celestial bodies until they can be studied in detail." Then there was this:

The planetary protection officer…would be responsible for ensuring humans don't contaminate space, and in turn, that extraterrestrial contaminants and organisms, if they exist, don't contaminate Earth. (CNBC, August 10, 2017)

No matter what your viewpoint is on this new NASA job, it is thought-provoking to note that they have developed a job of this type, with a salary starting at six figures. Where is the JUSTICE LEAGUE when you need them?

Another thing that continually sparks interest and controversy over the existence of extraterrestrial life on other planets is the fact that UFO sightings not only continue to be reported but continue at an accelerated rate. In everyday America, it is difficult to find someone that doesn't at least know someone that has had a "close encounter" of some kind. *Close Encounters of a Third Kind* is another movie that personalized the idea of extraterrestrials and human beings interacting with each other. ET was presented as a very lovable entity, and the movie played on our sympathy for the poor little alien stranded here on earth. The movie *Star Wars*, brings this empathy and even sympathy to a mechanical hunk of metal. Through all the *Star Wars* sequels, and then the prequels, our culture has been introduced, and then desensitized to the idea of having real meaningful relationships with robots. This humanization of robots, along with never-ending advances in technology, is bringing the concept of having personal relationships with robots to a "science fiction meets reality" moment. As we see interest growing in robotics and artificial intelligence, we also find many who cannot wait to make contact with extraterrestrials of all types.

On the other hand, there is a small group of scientists, who were led by Stephen Hawking that have warned us about our relentless search for extraterrestrial life. Hawking's most recent warnings made just before his death, about our expanding search of the stars reminds me of an old *Twilight Zone* episode. The name of the episode was "Serving Mankind." The creatures from outer space that came to visit the small American town in this particular episode, were intent on pampering the humans with whom they came in contact. The residents of the town were in the dark about the real intentions of these extraterrestrial visitors. Then, someone found a book in the alien spacecraft. It was called "Serving Mankind," and as you might have guessed, it wasn't a manifesto of how they would bring kindness and a leisure lifestyle to the residents of the town, but rather it was a cookbook. Hawking warned that we may not like what or who we are visited by if we continue this reckless attempt to make contact with extraterrestrial beings. Whether it be human eating extraterrestrials that seem to come in peace but are more interested in cultivating a new food source, or terrorizing extraterrestrial robots programed to kill all living things that threaten their kind, the idea Hawking raised sounds like excellent material for an up-coming sci-fi horror movie. Stephen Hawking's warning aside, the governments of the world seem determined to do everything they can to make contact with any and all extraterrestrial life.

Along with the increasing interest in searching for alien life wherever it might exist in the universe, the search for new solar systems and planets that can support life is also accelerating. Astronomers are capable of reaching deeper and deeper into space with their telescopes and have been rewarded with the discoveries of new solar systems that contain "inhabitable planets." This, predictably, has shifted the search for extraterrestrial life into warp drive. As we have previously pointed out, the problem is; what is the definition of "inhabitable planets"? If we take the 1950s or '60s definition of *inhabitable*, the bar is set very low.

Woven in, out, and through the entire fabric of this *alien frenzy* is an evolving idea that many of the past ancient accounts of angels and other supernatural encounters in diverse cultures may have actually been encounters with extraterrestrials. The premise begins with the idea that Earth is nothing more than a breeding ground for extraterrestrials. And because of their advanced intelligence, they seemed to be supernatural to our ancient ancestors. That somewhere in the past, extraterrestrials came to this planet and either bred with some type of *Homo sapiens* that existed here or started an entire new race on the planet. Then the theory goes on to say that for thousands and thousands of years, these extraterrestrials, who are our biological ancestors, have watched over us from above and below. A branch of this theory contends that the Greek and Roman mythological gods were extraterrestrials that came to earth. Proponents of these theories point to many artifacts that have been around for thousands of years, and they point to the unexplainable ability of our ancestors several thousands of years ago to understand the movements of the stars and planets. They point to the fact that almost every civilization, going back as far as you want in written history, has some form of what we call the zodiac.

These depictions of the twelve constellations, although there are some differences, are amazingly similar throughout the world. This some say, lends credence to the idea that they were all given to the different civilizations and cultures of the world by visiting extraterrestrials. Anyone that takes a reasonable look at our zodiac, and compares the people and animals corresponding to the constellations, will note that there is no resemblance. You don't go out into the night sky, look up at Orion, and see a hunter with his bow and arrow, unless you have seen that depiction somewhere else. The resemblance is just not there. Do you see a fish in the constellation Pisces? Do you really see two people in the constellation Gemini? Of course not. So where did all these like images come from in so many different cultures throughout the world? ANCIENT ASTRONAUT THEORIESTS say they came from extraterrestrials.

So what can we say about all of this? It's difficult to dismiss the whole idea as fantasy because of these physical, material objects and drawings we find here on our planet. There are structures, drawings on cave walls, and huge drawings on the earth that can only be seen from the air. There are what seem to be large ancient landing strips in remote parts of Central and South America, as well as in the Orient. There have been giant "human" skeletons uncovered, with double rows of teeth remaining in their skulls, in several different parts of the world. There are architectures made of stones so large modern equipment couldn't lift them and seem to have been cut by lasers. Lasers were obviously not in existence at the time they were built, according to our history. There are places on this earth that at one time seem to have had strange unexplained and powerful energy sources. There must be some explanation for these things. It seems that in this modern-day Babylon, one of the only explanations being offered is that there must be some extraterrestrial alien race of beings that is responsible for them.

But is it possible that the answers have been here all along? Is it possible that millions of people have read the explanation of these mysteries and just haven't understood? Is it possible that God Himself gave us the answers long, long ago and we are just now at a point where we can see and understand the truth? We're going to examine these questions and more and will try to find some answers. And maybe, we can find what we're looking for in the Holy Scriptures themselves.

We will explore many of the physical objects that exist on this planet, and please make no mistake their existence is undeniable. We are going to examine these physical objects, located all over the world on many different continents, and then look at how they fit into what we are told in the Bible. Today on television, there are programs being watched by millions of people that highlight these amazing physical places and objects like the pyramids, amazing rock carvings all over the world, and other various unexplainable remains. Then, on these television programs the ANCIENT ASTRONAUT THEORIESTS raise the possibility that extraterrestrials are responsible for them.

New discoveries are continually being made such as the underwater cities recently discovered in the Aegean Sea and off the coast of Japan near Okinawa and in the Gulf of Cambay off the western coast of India. These underwater cities can't be explained by current mainstream science and are used by the ANCIENT ASTRONAUT THEORIESTS to bolster their claims. Many of these structures and carvings, above and below water, date back thousands and thousands of years—way before our written history even began. Sometimes, they date much farther back in time than mainstream science is even willing to admit is possible. We will look at the evidence these structures were inhabited long before modern-day science claims intelligent life existed on this planet, and how that stacks up with the accounts given in the Bible.

ANCIENT ASTRONAUT THEORIESTS raise the possibility that legends of old, like the Greek and Roman gods were extraterrestrial beings. In like manner, the possibility is raised that the giants of the Bible may have been extraterrestrial beings from another planet. In fact, the idea that the angels described in the Bible could have been extraterrestrial beings is also being floated by the ANCIENT ASTRONAUT THEORIESTS. Very few Christians have any idea what the Bible says about these things, biblical illiteracy runs rampant today.

CHAPTER 2

The Pyramids of Egypt and Stonehenge

There has been much written over the years, about the Egyptian pyramids, but most people don't realize there are tremendous differences between the many pyramids found in Egypt. There are approximately eighty Egyptian pyramids in all, but the three Pyramids of Giza are the most famous and the most important. The Great Pyramid of Giza is the largest of these three pyramids and is the oldest and by far the most unusual of the three. The two smaller pyramids, which are now in almost total ruin, were probably the first copies of the first and largest pyramid. The other pyramids in Egypt are most likely later inferior copies of the first three and were used as burial tombs. There is no evidence, however that the three Pyramids of Giza were ever used as burial tombs. This of course begs the question, what was the purpose of these stone structures? It should be noted that only one manmade structure originally designated as one of the "Seven Ancient Wonders of the World" still exists; that would be the Great Pyramid of Giza.

According to the historian Herodotus, the Great Pyramid was built in the Fourth Egyptian Dynasty by its second king Khufu (Cheops) who reigned for fifty years. The historian adds that the pharaoh's brother Cephren rained another fifty-six years totaling 106 years during which the Great Pyramid was built. History tells us that during this period the Egyptians suffered many calamities and for many years its temples were closed. According to Corey's Ancient Fragments, it was at this time the Shepherd Kings arrived in Egypt and helped complete the Great Pyramid of Giza. I think it is more likely they were involved in helping the Egyptians complete the two smaller pyramids; I do not believe the Great Pyramid was built at this time or that it was built by the Egyptians.

The noted church historian, Archbishop Ussher, referred to the migration of the Shepherd Kings from Arabia to Egypt in his chronology. The Shepherd Kings seem to have exerted their power upon the Egyptian culture and caused the closing of their idolatrous temples. They are credited with the construction of the Great Pyramid and for starting a new religion in Egypt, which worshiped the One Almighty God. According to ancient historians, these "foreign people" left Egypt and upon their departure great rejoicing took place among the Egyptians. With the Shepherd Kings' restraints removed, the Egyptian people returned to their worship of idols. We know from the Bible that Joseph was sold into slavery in Egypt and became Pharaoh's governor over the entire country. The Bible also tells us that Joseph, through God's visions, saved the people of Egypt from starvation by storing up food for seven years, and at the end of seven years when the famine began, Joseph's father, Jacob, and his entire family was taken in by Pharaoh and weathered the storm in Egypt. I believe this family, the root of Israel, was the group that became known as the Shepherd King's, and if that is true, you can be sure they did not build the Great Pyramid.

An important little-known fact about the ancient Egyptian people that sometimes gets clouded because of the Shepherd Kings is that Egyptians didn't raise sheep. The Egyptians of that time ate goat and pig and preferred linen to wool. The Shepherd Kings brought sheep to Egypt and because of them, mutton and wool became available in the area. We can only speculate, but it would seem that when Jacob and his family moved to Egypt they had a huge impact on the religious practices of the Egyptian people. Remember, Joseph was running the country and it was widely known that his visions from the One Almighty God was what saved the entire country from starvation. It would stand to reason the people of Egypt would become subservient to Joseph's God while he was in power. It is also obvious that when Jacob's bones and the rest of his family returned to their homeland, the Egyptian people returned to their idol worshiping ways.

Exploration of the Great Pyramid began in 1721 by Nicholas Shaw and then later by Napoleon's army when the French were defeated in 1798. Over the centuries, many drawings and diagrams have been made of the Great Pyramid of Giza. Although the Great Pyramid of Giza is almost solid rock, there are several passageways that run through it and into inter-chambers. The English astronomer, Sir John Hershel, was convinced that the Great Pyramid was an illustration of advanced design and construction. Hershel believed the pyramid was evidence of an advanced knowledge of astronomy, applied mathematics, and other scientific understanding. He believed this advanced knowledge demonstrated in the pyramid predated our modern knowledge by several thousand years. Several years later, a London publisher named John Taylor, who was gifted in mathematics and astronomy, began to measure the Great Pyramid to analyze it from a mathematical point of view. The Great Pyramid was later explored by a professor-astronomer from Scotland, named Piazzi Smyth, who published a three-volume record of his results.

The location of the Great Pyramid is telling; it is placed precisely so it divides equally the Earth's terrain. Because of the high degree of accuracy in orienting the building to true north, it is obvious the architect knew how to locate the poles of the earth. Many experts claim that the Great Pyramid is more perfectly oriented than we could achieve today with all our modern technology. The Great Pyramid of Giza is also an enormous sundial sitting in the desert of Egypt. It is not only accurate for determining days and hours but also the seasons of the year. Just as a modern chronometer gives the hours of the day, so too the Great Pyramid accurately gives the day upon which winter solstice, spring equinox, summer solstice, and autumn equinox occur.

Knowledge of astronomy and applied mathematics are not the only amazing ancient scientific understanding demonstrated in the Great Pyramid. The stones that make up the Great Pyramid are largely composed of coarse limestone. It is estimated that over 2 million limestone blocks were used in the construction of the Great Pyramid of Giza, and it is believed they were quarried from the Giza Plateau. The gigantic size and weight of these building blocks and how they were transported to the building site is difficult to comprehend. The precision and angles at which they were cut is a challenge to duplicate even today. The space between the gigantic stones in most places is thinner than a sheet of aluminum foil. Perhaps most mysterious of all is the extremely thin layer of white cement used to glue the original facing to the limestone blocks. The glue was so strong that broken pieces of limestone have been found, which still have the facing firmly affixed to it because of this amazing ancient adhesive. Modern science has not been able to duplicate this ancient cement.

ANCIENT ASTRONAUT THEORIESTS believe that the Great Pyramid of Giza was an ancient power plant. Modern examination of the tunnels and chambers within the Great Pyramid shows that chemical reactions took place within the pyramid, and this suggests electrical power was created. A water system under the pyramid is thought to have created a turbulence that would enhance the chemical process taking place inside. ANCIENT ASTRONAUT THEORIESTS also believe that the alignment of the Great Pyramid with many monoliths across the globe suggests that the power being created could be distributed worldwide in a wireless fashion. They point to the missing capstone on the Great Pyramid and theorize the mechanism involved in the transmission of the electrical power is missing. Similar devices they say were at one time mounted on top of the many monoliths across the globe that are aligned perfectly with the Great Pyramid. It is also believed by the ANCIENT ASTRONAUT THEORIESTS that some great calamity or catastrophe must have taken place which destroyed them.

One of the great questions raised by ANCIENT ASTRONAUT THEORISTS is how the construction of the Great Pyramid was possible. They point out that some experts estimate that 50 million inhabitants of Egypt would have been necessary for construction during the time of the building of the Great Pyramid. They also point out that even if there were only one-tenth of that number necessary for construction, it would have been impossible to feed that many people. They ask an important question: "Where, while surrounded by the great Egyptian deserts, would you be able to find enough food to feed that many people?"

Would it surprise you that the Great Pyramid of Giza is mentioned in the Bible? It shouldn't; a structure that great, in a civilization so intermingled with the Israelites, it would be surprising if it wasn't mentioned. Jeremiah 32 states,

> 20 Which hast set signs and wonders in the land
> of Egypt, even unto this day...

In the book of Isaiah 19, in what is believed to be End Time prophecy, it states,

> 19 In that day shall there be an altar to the Lord
> in the midst of the land of Egypt, and a pillar at
> the border there of to the Lord.

> 20 And it shall be for a sign and for a witness
> unto the Lord of the hosts in the land of Egypt:
> for they shall cry unto the Lord because of the
> oppressors, and he shall send them a savior, and a
> great one, and he shall deliver them.

According to this Bible verse, this monument-altar is to be found "in the midst of the land of Egypt" and yet will be "at the border there of." This seems to be some ancient riddle of God. But the truth is, there is only one spot on the face of the globe where those conditions were exactly true, and that spot is where the Great Pyramid of Giza stands. The pyramid not only sits exactly in the geometric center of Egypt but also on what was at one time the border between the Pharaoh kingdom of Egypt and the Shepherd Kings kingdom of Egypt. It also stands on the southern extremity, or border, of the Nile-Delta quadrant. Perhaps the most convincing evidence that this stone monument once sat on the boundary between these two kingdoms, at the same time it sits in the center of Egypt is found in its title, Great Pyramid of Giza, means Great Pyramid of the Border.

Pyramids are megaliths that are closely related to monoliths, and we are no stranger to monoliths here in the United States; in fact one of our most famous national monuments is a monolith. The Washington Monument was built in the nineteenth century to commemorate the first president of the United States, George Washington. It stands 555 feet above America's capital city Washington, DC, and with its distinctive pyramid shape, the Washington Monument is considered the tallest stone obelisk in the world. The word *obelisk* is a generic term used for rectangular shaped pillars with pointed tops that are found throughout Egyptian structures as well as in many other cultures. Most have writing or pictographs on them, and they often record special events, record the entire reigns of different kings and rulers, and often record famous and important battles. Although the Washington Monument looks identical to other obelisks across the globe, it is not. The Washington Monument is built out of blocks of stone; the ancient obelisks are different because they are one piece of solid stone. These massive standing stones are known as monoliths and millions of them were used to construct monuments across the ancient world, including locations that include Turkey, Peru, Egypt, Ethiopia, and Indonesia. The mystery of monoliths has always been twofold; how were they constructed and what was their purpose?

Stonehenge, located in Wiltshire, England, about ninety miles outside of London, and two miles to the west of Amesbury, consists of a ring of standing stones. Stonehenge is a prehistoric monument whose stones stand approximately thirteen feet high, are about seven feet wide, and weigh about twenty-five tons each. According to archaeologists, Stonehenge was constructed sometime between 3000 BC and 2000 BC. Experts using radiocarbon dating have determined the monoliths date back to around four thousand years ago. This time several thousand years ago is called the megalithic period and is defined by the fact that our ancestors, in almost every part of the civilized world, began to build these gigantic stone structures called monoliths. These cultures, which are known as megalithic cultures, are still something of a mystery. Why at this point in history do we find civilizations all over the world begin to place great importance on these huge monoliths? Some of these monoliths are very exotic; many of them have rocks stacked on top of other rocks in very exotic ways. It is still a challenge to understand exactly why these gigantic stones were placed where they are. Additionally, some of the stones were transported from over one hundred miles away is it possible that these prehistoric people could accomplish such an enormous and seemingly impossible task?

At Stonehenge, the earthen bank and ditch surrounding it constitute the earliest phase of the monument, and has been dated to around 3100 BC. A circular earthwork was constructed at the site around 3000 BC. This circular earthwork consisted of a ditch that had an inner and outer bank. Inside the bank were fifty-six holes, which became known as the Aubrey Holes, named after John Aubrey who'd identified them in 1666. Around 2500 BC, more construction took place at the site where two types of stones were placed at the center of the monument; these were large sarsens and smaller bluestones.

In the beginning, Stonehenge could have been a burial ground since human remains have been found that date back as early as 3000 BC. Mike Parker Pearson led a team of archaeologists that excavated parts of Stonehenge in 2013. More than fifty thousand cremated bones were found buried at Stonehenge; these remains had originally been buried in individual holes. Experts believe, the last new construction at Stonehenge took place around 1600 BC, and the last time it was used for animal sacrifice was sometime during the Iron Age. It has been estimated that at times more than four thousand people gathered at Stonehenge for the Midwinter and Midsummer festivals each year.

The mystery of Stonehenge endures undaunted by time. The construction techniques used by Stonehenge builders are still unknown. Conventional techniques such as sheer legs, or rolling logs, are often cited as possible methods, but all methods seem lacking, considering the gigantic size and weight of these stones. Some modern attempts have been made at duplicating the feat of moving just one of these huge stones. One such experiment conducted in 1995 claimed success, but even it has its critics. In the year 2000, a similar experiment was conducted using only Stone Age tools and Stone Age methods. This Welsh group experienced several problems, and at one point the stone being transported was dropped into the water while being carried between two rowboats on a sling. That entire project was eventually scrapped.

A whiff of the supernatural surrounds Stonehenge, and it is propagated in its legends and folklore. Many experts such as Professor Geoffrey Wainwright of the Society of Antiquaries of London believe that Stonehenge was a place of healing. They compare it to the legendary healing site of Lourdes and argue that this would account for the high number of burials in the area. They say the evidence of trauma and deformity in some of the remains supports this theory. Another Geoffrey, Geoffrey of Monmouth, wrote about Stonehenge in the early twelfth century. Geoffrey of Monmouth claimed that Stonehenge was erected as a memorial to hundreds of Britons who were slain by the Saxons. Additionally, he wrote that the wizard Merlin directed that the stones for the monument be procured from the "Giants' Ring," a stone circle with magical healing powers said to be located somewhere in Ireland. The great twentieth-century French philosopher Jean Marcel wrote forty books on Merlin, King Arthur, and all their mid-evil escapades. One thing Marcel was always unwavering about was his belief that Merlin was a real person. He believed Merlin possessed incredibly powerful, almost supernatural ability and came to mankind to be their teacher of things beyond the grasp of normal humans. ANCIENT ASTRONAUT THEORISTS believe, the stories of Merlin and King Author's court are proof that extraterrestrial entities contacted our ancestors in the ancient past.

Many believe that the composition of the stone used in building these monoliths act as a medium. We know the properties of these stones have been found to have certain effects on the human body, through vibration and other unseen properties that are believed to have healing effects. The stones have spectacular properties of toughness and hardness and some of their other properties, such as quartz crystals, are thought to also have healing qualities in many different cultures. Many experts believe, Stonehenge was a healing place where people came with their ailments to be cured.

Others argue that Stonehenge was nothing more than a burial ground in the beginning. Archaeologists estimate Stonehenge was the home to over 150 cremation burials between 3000 BC and 2300 BC, and it's known as Britain's biggest cemetery of that time period. Stonehenge began to be revived as a site of religious significance during the twentieth century. As recently as the year of this writing, religious groups who are mostly pagan at their roots make their pilgrimage to Stonehenge. Some Druids have even recreated Stonehenge in other parts of the world as a form of their Druidism worship.

One thing we know for sure about Stonehenge is that its layout was not done by chance. Looking at Stonehenge from the air in what is believed to be its original pristine state gives us real food for thought. Seen from the air, Stonehenge is an actual replica of our solar system, and all those concentric circles represent planets in our solar system. How did they know this? How did they have any idea about our solar system at this ancient time? ANCIENT ASTRONAUT THEORIESTS believe this information was given to our ancestors by extraterrestrials. Stonehenge also seems to be a calendar that helped ancient cultures know the correct times to plant. Its alignment also is designed to predict lunar and solar eclipses as well as the occurrence of winter solstice, spring equinox, summer solstice, and autumn equinox. ANCIENT ASTRONAUT THEORIESTS contend Stonehenge was a landing location for ancient space aliens and insist records show the location has always had a high number of reported UFO sighting.

CHAPTER 3

Other Monoliths

Avebury

Stonehenge has been called the most architecturally sophisticated ancient stone circle, but the largest of them is Avebury, located about twenty miles north of Stonehenge. Experts say Avebury was constructed between 2850 BC and 2200 BC, and today it consists of a massive circular bank and ditch enclosing 28.5 acres. The area is so large at one time there was an entire village built inside the circle. Inside the ditch is an inner stone circle that encloses two smaller stone circles. Originally, this circle was composed of at least ninety-eight stones, but now only twenty-seven remain. From excavation and soil studies, it is thought that the three rings originally contained at least 154 stones of which only thirty-six remain standing today. The stones are huge, some weigh between twenty and fifty tons apiece in this great circle. During the Medieval era, it is believed several of the stones were knocked over and buried by local Christians who believed they were pagan symbols. Then in the seventeenth and eighteenth centuries, still more of the remaining stones were removed. Later, some of the stones were broken up and used as building materials. The site was purchased in the 1930s by archaeologist Alexander Keiller, heir to a large British fortune. Keiller cleared away the old structures on the property and repositioned many of the stones. Avebury is the largest known circular monolith in the world, and as with Stonehenge, the method of its construction and purpose are up for debate.

The general outline of the Avebury temple was still visible early into the eighteenth century, but in the 1720s, local farmers unaware of the cultural and architectural value of the ancient temple continued with the destruction of the site. Dr. William Stukeley was the first to clearly recognize that the original ground plan of Avebury was a representation of the body of a serpent passing through a circle, thus forming a traditional alchemical symbol. The enormous head and tail of the serpent were delineated by fifty-foot-wide avenues of standing stones, each of the avenues reaching a mile and a half into the countryside. One of the avenues connected Avebury to another stone circle known as the Sanctuary. Many other massive earthen stone monuments have been discovered scattered around the Avebury complex. In another direction, about 1,500 meters south of the Avebury circles, stands Silbury Hill, which is the largest megalithic construction in Europe. Silbury Hill is said to be the greatest manmade mound in Europe and harbors a burial chamber dating back perhaps six thousand years.

ANCIENT ASTRONAUT THEORIESTS contend that these stones were very important to this ancient culture and were used to find some type of rhyme and rhythm in their cycles of planting and life in general. They point out that when there is stability in the world, chaos and disorder cannot dominate life, and they believe that Avebury was a meeting place significant to religious rituals conducted at the time, attempting to maintain a connection with their ancestors from the stars. According to these researchers, there must have been a profound purpose for the way this circle of stone was aligned at Avebury, perhaps involving celestial beings that once visited the site thousands of years earlier. The area around Avebury has always been associated with a kind of mystery and magic, there have been many UFO sightings in the area, as well as ghost sightings and hundreds of crop circles in this region.

Avebury mythologies always point to the sky and celestial beings, the shining ones as they were called, descended from the sky and educated people in various disciplines such as agriculture, mathematics, geometry, and engineering. It is thought that Avebury and other giant megaliths were set up by ancient people, perhaps by extraterrestrials who went out and surveyed the wilderness lands of earth. While surveying, they set up these gigantic stone survey markers. Then, for some unknown reason, they placed these large stones in circles like at Avebury. At Avebury it is clear someone fenced off an environment where perhaps only certain people were allowed inside. And according to ANCIENT ASTRONAUT THEORIESTS, there may have been a profound purpose for this circle alignment of stones, one that perhaps connected the participants to celestial beings. The area around Avebury has always been associated with magic and mystery. ANCIENT ASTRONAUT THEORIESTS suggest that maybe these ancient inhabitants of Avebury thought they could communicate with the deities through these monolithic stones. If so, they say, this might explain why man has been drawn to stone structures throughout the world since ancient times.

Lyon Rock

Around the area of Sigiriya, Sri Lanka, there is a natural monolith that towers 660 feet over the surrounding landscape, it is better known as Lyon Rock. This monolith was discovered in 1831 by a British Army officer named Jonathan Forbes. Forbes discovery is a natural monolith, a giant cliff, and it has stairs cut into it, and a beautiful ancient palace had been built on its top. This palace was built in a very remote area that is high up on top of this monolith. At one time, it was certainly a Buddhist monastery from the first millennium BC, and then around 500 AD, it is believed it became a fortress and palace for a local king. On top of the monolith are gardens and grounds that span the entire top of the rock. There are also various caves on this monolith and within these caves are several different murals. These fresco paintings feature portraits of women, and some researchers insist they represent ladies of the king's court at that time. Others, however, suggest that these women are more likely religious figures.

According to ANCIENT ASTRONAUT THEORIESTS, these fresco paintings reveal evidence that extraterrestrials contacted these people in the distant past. Many of these paintings depict people emerging from the clouds; some seem to be floating in midair. These researchers wonder what the ancient artists were trying to depict in these murals. According to local myth, Lyon Rock was created by the gods who descended from the stars. ANCIENT ASTRONAUT THEORIESTS contend that ancient space travelers visited these people and these paintings are attempts to depict these aliens. The ancients believed these monoliths were gateways between our world and the world of the gods. In Sigiriya, we find the same concept, obviously in many cultures a monolith can be very important and sacred to the people. It was believed in cultures throughout the world at the time, and still to this day in some areas that ascending up to the heights of the mountains provided a path-way of reaching out and communicating with the spiritual world.

In ancient Buddhist cultures, Mt. Meru is the name used to describe a cosmic mountain. Mt. Meru is described in ancient literature as a mass of golden light, a blazing golden fire in the shape of a mountain. Mt. Meru is believed by Buddhists to be at the center of the universe and exists not in a physical sense but in an energy sense. It is their belief that the gods lived upon the mountains and built palaces and cities there. The ancient people believed Mt. Meru was a place of connection and communication with the gods themselves and was the point of access between our world and heaven. The Sigiriya area has been referred to as a small-scale replica of Mt. Meru where the ancients created a specific place, in their specific time, where they could establish an uplink and downlink to the gods in the heavens.

Easter Islands

Easter Island sits isolated in the Pacific Ocean some two thousand miles west of Chile. On this mysterious tiny island stand nearly nine hundred monolithic stone statues that have huge heads and torsos that are carved out of volcanic rock. These statues are called Moai, and they stand approximately thirty feet tall and some weigh up to seventy-five tons. At first glance, you don't realize that some of these statues are buried right up to their chests. That means these statues are two or three times larger than they look to be sticking out of the ground. The statues look inward toward the center of the island and up toward the sky. Many visitors say that standing next to them on the ground, the tendency is to join them and look toward the heavens. The statues are obviously interested in something that is happening in the sky and must have been very important to the people that erected them.

Archaeologists tell us the native Polynesian inhabitants of Easter Island, known as the Rapa Nui people, constructed the Moai between the twelfth and eighteenth centuries AD to honor their ancestors. But recently, archaeological excavations have revealed that the figures were naturally buried over a long period of time, and this would seem to disprove this dating. This seems to support the theory that certain people came to Easter Island, where they carved and erected these monoliths long before the twelfth century AD. Some believe it is reasonable to assume that these figures represent those that were the original builders. If the Moai are older than previously thought, who really built them and why? The Rapa Nui are thought to have arrived on Easter Island no earlier than 300 AD. Is it possible that celestial beings visited Easter Island thousands of years ago?

ANCIENT ASTRONAUT THEORISTS believe these monolithic figures provide evidence that the Rapa Nui's ancestors were ancient space travelers. There is no argument that the faces of these statues do not look like East Islanders. Eric von Daniken is fond of describing them as looking like robots with long narrow noses and narrow lips. He points out that these statues have no physical characteristics in common with the Rapa Nui people. Von Daniken also points out that they have elongated heads that are very similar to those cone-shaped skulls we see in Mexico and Egypt, as well as other areas in the world. So who are these people? ANCIENT ASTRONAUT THEORISTS contend that one possible explanation of why these statues look toward the heavens is because they are pointing us toward the place of their origin and encouraging humans not to forget from where they came. Could it really be possible that the Moai represent extraterrestrial beings pointing us toward their heavenly origin?

Indonesian Monoliths

In Indonesia close to the Bada Valley, hidden in the isolated mountains of the island of Sulawesi, there are more than twenty monoliths scattered throughout the fields of this farming region. These statues are said to date back to the first millennium BC, but their actual date of creation has never been definitively determined. Much of this valley is covered with rice terraces, which are common throughout Indonesia and Southeast Asia, but here in the middle of these rice patties sit these statues. Obviously, the question is, how did these giant boulders, each weighing one hundred tons or more, get transported up from the deep river valleys of this region, which are many miles away? And why would you transport these giant boulders up into the valley, erect them, and then carve them into giant statues? Even more mysterious than this is how could the monoliths we find halfway around the globe on Easter Island bear such a close resemblance to these found on the island of Sulawesi? ANCIENT ASTRONAUT THEORISTS believe that the inspiration came from the same extraterrestrial visitors. They point out that you find similar carvings styles of these strange alien-looking faces, which are very systematic, and beautifully carved in many different places. They contend that the similarities, found in monoliths in different parts of the world, resemble characteristics they have seen in extraterrestrials who they considered to be gods.

Experts claim these carved megaliths are between one thousand and five thousand years old, and when the locals are asked about the origin of these statues, they explain that they've always been there. They are believed by some to have been used in different types of worship that involved human sacrifice, and others believe that the statues were erected to ward off evil spirits. One of the local legends claims that the statues are criminals that had been turned to stone to warn others of wrong doing. There is even a superstition that the statues can disappear and appear again at different places, there have been reports of the statues being found in slightly different locations from time to time. It is also mysterious that the specific type of stone used to make the Indonesia monoliths is not found anywhere in the local area.

Gunung Padang is a megalithic site located in Karyamukti village in the West Java Province. It's about fifty kilometers southwest of the city of Cianjur. Some call it the largest megalithic site in all of Southeast Asia. This massive Indonesian site was put on the international map when it was reported in the publication Rapporten van de Oudheidkundige Dienst (Report of the Department of Antiquities) in 1914. The Dutch historian N. J. Krom also mentioned it in 1949, and employees of the National Archeology Research Centre studied the site in 1979. This site covers a hill that has a series of terraces bordered by retaining walls of stone. It has about four hundred andesite steps and is covered with massive rectangular stones. Indonesian culture considers the site sacred, and they believe King Siliwangi built the structure in one single night. The structure faces northwest, toward the Mt. Gede volcano, and it is estimated that the site was completed around 5000 BC. There is speculation that the entire hill may itself be an ancient pyramid. Researchers tell us by using modern testing techniques, there is a structure beneath the surface with large chambers, and many manmade artifacts have been discovered at the site.

The construction of the site dates to 6,500 years BC, and the artifacts at the surface date to about 4,800 years BC. It is interesting to note that the walls of the terraces resemble those found at Machu Picchu in Peru. Dr. Danny Hillman Natawidjaja, who currently works at the Lab Earth, RC Geotechnology, Indonesian Institute of Sciences, is responsible for the archaeological team that investigated the site, they announced the discovery of a metal device that is presumed to be the world's oldest electrical instrument. According to researchers, this object is made of gold and copper and seems to resemble a primitive capacitor. Finding an electrical device in that area suggests that ancient man mastered electricity thousands of years ago. Researchers also found giant bowls, springs, domes, towers, aquifers and a transmitter. Notably, magnetic anomalies are also found in these locations. ANCIENT ASTRONAUT THEORISTS suggest that somehow these statues, strewn across Indonesia, were allowing the people to commemorate or maybe even communicate with some entities. They were memorials to the gods, the deities who were once here on this earth. They suggest it is possible these monoliths were created by mankind to pay homage to actual otherworldly beings who visited Earth in a distant past. And they believe monoliths throughout the world have a profound connection to each other.

Stone Spheres

Some of the most interesting monolithic remains from ancient times are the stone balls that are found all across the world. There are the small spheres, finely carved with ornate drawings, from which an appreciation of the ancient art and design of the time can be realized. The precision and near-perfect roundness of these spheres is amazing. But the stone spheres that really boggles the mind, even more than the spheres of India and the Orient, are those stone balls found in the jungles of Costa Rica. There is an assortment of over three hundred of these spheres strung across the Diquís Delta and on Isla del Caño, in Costa Rica they are called Las Bolas, which means "the balls," in Spanish. In 2014, UNESCO added the pre-Columbian chiefdom settlements with their stone spheres of rock to their list of world heritage sites.

Spheres are one thing that do not normally occur in nature. The craftsmanship and accuracy of these carvings are unexplainable, considering the time they were done. Although some experts disagree, a few have claimed that some of the balls are so perfectly round, they could not be duplicated today with modern tools. The spheres range in size from very small to over two meters in diameter and some are estimated to weigh more than fifteen tons. Over decades of research, experts seem to agree that the spheres were made by hammering natural boulders with other rocks, and then polishing the boulder with sand. The quality of the monoliths varies greatly, leading some people to theorize that this area was a school to teach the art of sphere making.

In the 1930s, the property upon which the spheres are located was purchased by United Fruit Company and the spheres were discovered as they cleared the jungle for banana plantations. John Hoopes, associate professor of Anthropology and Director of the

Global Indigenous Nations Studies Program at the University of Kansas has examined the spheres closely. According to the professor, the stones were not scientifically reported until the 1930s when the United Fruit Company began clearing land in Costa Rica for banana plantations. The professor explains that dating the spheres based on the age of archeological deposits found around the spheres won't give you the date they were made; only when those things left around it were made, he says it is very difficult to reach an exact date of when they were made.

There are many myths surrounding the spheres; some say they were huge play toys for giants. Other myths attribute these spheres to the lost city of Atlantis or weapons of the gods that were used to drive away the gods of thunder and hurricanes. Measurements of these stone spheres has been difficult because of the conditions, and because in many cases, the balls are at least half buried in the ground. Many believe that they are buried because over the years, sediment has built up around them. Many of the stones have been removed from where they were originally found so the wealthy of the area could display them at their homes and in their gardens. Sadly, this destroyed much of the information about their origin and their original placement within the context of the entire area. Mystery continues to surround the stone spheres of Costa Rica. ANCIENT ALIEN THEORISTS believe that these giant balls were used to represent different stars and planets within our solar system. These balls would be rolled around, and rearranged, from time to time to represent changes in the night sky. This theory seems reasonable considering the ancients' fascination with the stars, planets, and our solar system.

As amazing as the Costa Rica stone balls are, it is just as amazing that stone spheres very similar to those in Costa Rica are found halfway across the world in a small town in Bosnia. Some of the stone spheres of Bosnia are maybe twice as large as those found in Costa Rica. Archaeologist Sam Osmanagich, known by some as the Bosnia Indiana Jones, estimates that some of the balls may weigh as much as thirty-five tons. The reference to Indiana Jones comes from the movie *Raiders of the Lost Ark*, where giant stone balls are seen rolling down ramps as Harrison Ford attempts to avoid ultimate destruction. The Bosnia balls seem to be just as perfectly round as those found in Costa Rica, and the Bosnia Indiana Jones presents an interesting theory concerning these stone spheres. Osmanagich offers the theory that these huge stone balls were formed while in a liquid state. He theorizes that huge molds were used, and through some advanced process, the stone was turned into some type of molten lava and poured into the molds.

As in the case of the Costa Rican balls, dating the Bosnia stone spheres is very difficult. As in Costa Rica, the methodology used mostly relies on artifacts found around the stones, which may have been left thousands of years after the carving of the great stone spheres. In *Archaeological Park: Bosnian Pyramid of the Sun foundation*, a blog written by Osmanagich, he suggests the Bosnian balls could be the largest manmade stone balls in Europe, perhaps the world. Osmanagich says many other stone spheres found throughout the world could point to long-lost advanced civilizations from the distant past, of which we have no written records. He says, "They had high technology, different than ours." He then adds, "They knew the power of geometrical shapes, because the sphere is one of the most powerful shapes along with pyramidal and conical shapes..."

The country of Peru contains many ancient monoliths. In an ancient building in the ancient city of Tiahuanaco, there is a stone idol that experts estimate weighs about twenty tons and was carved from a single block of red sandstone. The estimated age of this gigantic stone idol is pre-Inca Indian, it is a mystery how the idol and the temple, which contains it were constructed, considering the primitive tools and techniques available at the time. The carving on the idol is exquisitely delicate and has been compared to work done on today's fine crystal. It is covered with hundreds of carved symbols, and the fine detail of the workmanship stands in stark contrast to its surroundings. In the book *The Great Idol of Tiahuanaco* by H. S. Bellamy and P. Allan, it is theorized that the symbols on the great Idol embody a mass of astronomical data about the heavens and earth as of twenty-seven thousand years ago. They believe the idol details a series of events that took place at that time. A large object was captured by Earth's gravity and, as it spun around and around, its mass and velocity caused the Earth's rotation to slow as well as its orbital velocity around the sun. According to this theory, the object captured by Earth's gravity, was making 425 orbits around the earth each year, and at that time one Earth year only amounted to 288 days. ANCIENT ASTRONAUT THEORISTS believe that the only possible explanation for this mammoth monolith is extraterrestrial intervention.

The countries of Peru, Bolivia, and Chile also contain many other ancient stone temples, in addition to the one that contains the Great Idol of Tiahuanaco. Located near the southern Bolivian shores of the sacred Lake Titicaca, Tiahuanaco was the capital of the Tiwanaku Empire, which dates to 1000 BC. There were two primary types of walls used in the construction, those with large irregular blocks, and those using finely fitting straight edge block construction. Huge blocks, some one hundred tons each, are topped with other blocks weighing more than sixty tons, to create the walls. The precision of some of the cut blocks point to the use of sophisticated tools and advanced instruments of measurement. The Kalasasaya is another sacred structure, measuring 120 by 130 meters. At the site, there are highly developed water conduits that seem to be extremely advanced for that time. There are severed stone heads protruding from the interior of the sandstone walls, which include regularly placed tall stone columns. In this area is found the Ponce Monolith, which is 3.5 meters tall, and is believed to depict a ruler, high priest, or the God of Tiwanaku. Perhaps the most famous structure of Tiwanaku is the Gateway of the Sun. This massive carved single block of andesite stone stands almost nine feet high and is over twelve feet wide. The top portion has forty-eight relief carvings of winged demons or angels, each carving with either a human or a bird head, wearing a feathered headdress. Under these figures can be seen a row of geometric figures, of what seems to be advanced math.

The culture of Tiwanaku was influenced by the imagery of its predecessors, and images at the site include the staff deity, winged creatures with bird heads, along with various severed trophy heads. The staff deity appears on the famous Gateway of the Sun showing a frontal view holding a staff in each hand, sunrays coming from the head, with a masked face and wearing a tunic, kilt, and belt. This same image is prevalent on much of the pottery and other architecture in the area. ANCIENT ASTRONAUT THEORISTS contend that this site was originally built by extraterrestrials. According to legend, the goddess Oryana came down from the stars in a golden flying ship and oversaw the building of the site.

Located in what is now the Urabamba Basin, Andes, Peru, was the ancient Inca capital of Cuzco, known as the navel of the earth. Although, most of the construction of the ancient Inca buildings located there were destroyed following the sacking by Pizarro in 1535, some of the foundations remain. Here stand carved stones like those found in Tiwanaku. A twenty-thousand-ton monolith adorned with carved stairways and thrones exists there. Most mysteriously, this huge single stone monolith is turned upside down, turned over 180 degrees from how it was obviously carved. Several tests of the area have been conducted, and some believe the results show evidence of an atomic explosion. The perfectly carved andesite stone, in addition to several other construction features, is noticeably like Egyptian architecture.

In addition to the many monoliths found in Peru, the Nazca Lines provide us with many more unanswered questions. The Nazca Lines are a series of large ancient geoglyphs found in the Nazca desert in southern Peru. The largest of these drawings is over 1,200 feet long and the Nazca Lines were designated as a UNESCO World Heritage Site in 1994. Experts believe the drawings were created sometime between 500 BC and 500 AD, however, many don't accept the validity of these dates. Some figures are very complex, while many are simple lines and geometric shapes. Over seventy of the designs represent animals, such as birds, fish, llamas, jaguars, monkeys, and human figures. Other designs include shapes of plants, trees, and flowers. Experts differ in interpreting the purpose of the designs, but in general, they believe they have some religious significance.

Because of the stable climate on the plateau, the lines have mostly been naturally preserved, but some extreme weather has altered the general designs. Although it has been accepted for many years that these drawings are only visible from an aircraft in the sky, some are currently arguing that portions are visible from surrounding foothills and other high places. ANCIENT ASTRONAUT THEORISTS argue this is absurd, and the totality of any one large drawing could only be viewed from the air. Joe Nickell, a prominent skeptic of ANCIENT ASTRONAUT THEORY, claims to have reproduced figures using tools and technology available to the Nazca people. Accepting Nickell's conclusions require the acceptance of the idea that these ancient Nazca people possessed advance geometric knowledge. In addition, he offers no answer to the question, "Why?"

And of course, there are many other similar mysteries throughout the world that are begging for exploration. The Island of Elephantine in the center of the Nile at Aswan, about which ancient texts state that the name was derived because the island resembles the shape of an elephant. The problem is, the shape of the island can only be seen from the air. The famed Iron Pillar of Delhi in India, which is known for its unexplainable construction from rust-resistant metals unknown to modern man. The Terrace of Baalbek in Greece, where the construction is of stone blocks more than sixty-five feet long and that weigh nearly two thousand tons apiece. The Lussac Cave Portraits, in southern France, which depict many animal and human images. Some experts date these back as far as fifteen thousand years ago. Amazingly, many seem to be dressed in modern clothing, and wearing modern type hats. The Roman era shipwreck dating back to the first century BC known as the Antikythera Wreck, discovered by sponge divers in 1900, yielded numerous statues, coins, and other artifacts dating back to the fourth century BC. Amongst these artifacts was found the corroded remnants of a device many believed to be a small-scale planetarium, a type of analog computer.

Perhaps the most earthshaking of these mysterious discoveries can now be found in the Berlin state library and is known as the Piri Reis Maps. Experts believe the maps were drawn, probably copied by Admiral Piri Reis around the year 1700. Over the years the maps have been examined by many experts, including Arlington H Mallory a respected civil engineer and later in 1957 by the Jesuit priest Father Limeham who was director of the Western Observatory and a cartographer for the US Navy.

The maps were found to be amazingly accurate considering their age and show the outline of mountain ranges in the Antarctic, which were not discovered until 1952. These mountains have been covered with ice for many hundreds of years. Skeptics point to errors and omissions within the outline of the Antarctic, but no one can explain these depictions without the use of modern technology. One of the criticisms of the Piri Reis Maps is the distortion that takes place as the view extends out from the Caribbean area. Many believe that these distortions are the same as would occur when an aerial photograph would be taken. In 1954, Harvard trained scientist Charles Hapgood of Keene State College of New Hampshire began to examine the maps with his class. Hapgood and his students spent seven years on the project and eventually published a book on the study called *Maps of the Ancient Sea Kings*. Their conclusions are again mind-boggling.

First, they concluded that in some cases, the information found on the maps was not confirmed until the middle of the twentieth century. Second, the maps were explicitly accurate especially regarding longitudes which neither mariners or mapmakers had access to during the seventeenth and eighteenth centuries. Third, some unknown civilization or culture that predated any civilization known so far to man, must have mapped North America, China, Greenland, South America, and Antarctica. Furthermore, at the time the maps were made Greenland and Antarctica were not covered with their millennial old ice caps. Finally, the advanced knowledge appearing on these maps somehow survived the destruction of this unknown civilization and the destruction of ancient depositories of knowledge such as the library at Alexandria. The burning unanswered question posed by von Daniken in his book *Chariots of the Gods*, which is still unanswered forty years later is how did Piri Reis know about Antarctica and its mountains in the sixteenth century?

CHAPTER 4

Giants

Giants have been part of legions and lore from the beginning of recorded history. Even the Bible speaks of giants who roamed the earth during the time of Noah and others; we'll investigate this more closely later. From Jack in the Beanstalk to the one-eyed giant of the *Iliad and the Odyssey*, we find stories about giants in almost every ancient culture across the globe. Today, giants are used effectively in advertising; an example is the Jolly Green Giant. Giants are seen regularly in science fiction movies and animations, such as The Hulk and Shrek. Is it a coincident they are all green? Maybe not, partly because of their greenness, giants have been relegated to the realm of fantasy and fairy tales. According to ANCIENT ASTRONAUT THEORISTS, this is the farthest thing from the truth. They believe that giants walked the earth and might be the discarded products of extraterrestrial experimentation in the development of modern man, or that they may be remains of extraterrestrials, or…? It so happens, there is some physical evidence that is impossible to dismiss.

Early human fossils discovered on the island of Java (Indonesia) in 1891 and 1892 were originally named *Meganthropus palaeojavanicus*. The name survives as a common nickname for the fossil but is not considered valid today amongst mainstream paleontologists. The fossils consist of several large jawbones and skull fragments, which some regard as belonging to giants. Some question whether Mega, as we will call the fossil, should be placed in the category of human. Some researchers believe that Mega is more related to the

Australopithecines and should be called *Australopithecus palaeojavanicus*. Although paleontologists are not sure how, most believe Mega is related to the ancient human ancestor *Homo erectus*. Some fossils were found but then lost during World War II, but from molds that were made we can estimate that Mega stood around eight feet tall and would have weighed around six hundred pounds. Additional jaw fragments were found in 1979 and again in 1993. These specimens were badly damaged but one interesting feature was a double temporal Ridge (sagittal crest) and a very thick nuchal ridge. These features suggest great jaw strength and lead many experts to lean on a crossbreeding theory.

Adding to the lore, some Australian researchers believe that Mega still roams the land in Australia today. Some giant stone tools have been found recently, and modern-day sightings of a creature in the outback of Australia are continually reported. Some researchers into Bigfoot have suggested that Mega and Bigfoot might be one in the same. The height and weight attributed to these fossils coincide with size and weight estimates based on Bigfoot sighting reports.

Two fossilized teeth were found in 1927 by a Canadian, Davidson Black, in Zhoukoudian near Beijing. Known as the Peking man, this specimen was determined as belonging to a class of ancient human. Several skullcaps were found at the same site in December 1929, and while they appear to be similar, they also seem slightly larger than the Java Man. Some believe that the Peking man is a transitional fossil between apes and humans, but other experts refuse to entertain this possibility, arguing that the Peking man was some type of Neanderthal. The fossil specimens were dated in 2009 at roughly 750,000 years old. Later discoveries in the thirties have been estimated to be between five hundred thousand and three hundred thousand years old. Several skulls and cranial fragments have been discovered over the years, and from these specimens it has been estimated that the brain size of these giants was huge. Most of the finds over the years have involved teeth, and to date the number is more than one thousand individual isolated teeth. The size of these tooth specimens support estimates that the skulls were huge, and some claim the brain sizes were also gigantic.

In the early part of 2018, the Stone Circle Research Program administered by Michael Tellinger, began to report findings being made by the group in a secluded area of South Africa. Tillinger says it seems they're dealing with large numbers of humanoid mud fossils in the area. Reportedly, the fossils being found would suggest a height range of fifteen feet tall to much taller. As of March 2018, the group has reportedly collected over thirty fossils, one of the most astounding finds to date, is what seems to be a gigantic fossilized shoulder blade of a large being. As this group is just getting started at the time of this writing, more news out of South Africa is expected.

In May 1912, burial mounds were found near Lake Delavan, Wisconsin. The dig site was overseen by Beloit College, and over two hundred mounds were examined providing classic examples of eighteenth-century Woodland Culture. But because the enormous size of the skeletons and elongated skulls found at the Wisconsin site did not fit into the textbook standard concept of world history, they have been largely ignored. The find was first reported in the *New York Times* on May 4, 1912, when eighteen skeletons were found by two brothers in Southwest Wisconsin. The Times reported that not only were the skeletons enormous, but they exhibited several strange and freakish features. The skeletal remains range from seven and a half feet tall to ten feet tall, and their skulls were much larger than anything seen in America up until then. They have double rows of teeth, six fingers, and six toes, and they seemed to be of at least two different races. In recent years, there have been over two hundred giant digs where giant skeletons have been found, but little has been reported about these finds. The consensus amongst nonscientist observers is that the lack of reporting on these finds is due largely to the fact that they seem to question or even disprove the theory of evolution.

In August 1891, the *New York Times* first reported that the Smithsonian Institute had discovered, on Lake Mills, near Madison, Wisconsin, several large monuments in the shape of pyramids. *The Times* reported that scientists estimated that the population at the time of the building of these "pyramidal monuments" must have been about two hundred thousand and that an elaborate system of defensive "works" was found including trenches and tunnels. It is interesting to note that these large pyramid shaped monuments are in the same vicinity in which the Smithsonian giant skeletons were found. In December 1897, the *New York Times* followed up with the report on the discovery of three large burial mounds around Maple Creek, Wisconsin. In these ruins a skeleton of a gigantic man was found, the bones measured from head to foot over nine feet and were in a good state of preservation. The Times reported; the skull of this skeleton was as large as a half bushel basket.

Over the past one hundred years, giant skulls and skeletal remains of giants have been found in Minnesota, Ohio, Kentucky, Illinois, Iowa, and New York. All these burial sites seem similar in several ways and are also like the well-known mounds of the "Mound Builder People." The mound building era of history spans a period of over five thousand years, approximately from 3500 BC to 1600 AD, and while experts in the field claim to have a solid historical understanding of the peoples who lived in North America during this period, these aforementioned discoveries seem to discount these claims.

ANCIENT ASTRONAUT THEORISTS claim that these skeletal remains found across the world are evidence of extraterrestrials either interbreeding with human life form on the planet or they could be extraterrestrial remains themselves. They point to what they call the "Great Smithsonian Cover Up," although some of the mound builder skeletons are certainly on display in a few remote places, they say the Smithsonian Institution has deliberately hid away many of these giant skeletons. Vine Deloria, a Native American author and professor of law says the nineteenth-century Smithsonian Institution created a one-way door through which uncounted bones passed never to be seen again. The professor believes many answers concerning the deep past may exist among those bones.

It's important to point out how much there is out there for which the scientific community has no answers. We live in a time of science that I compare to the 1500s. We live in a time when scientists run around telling us they have figured out everything from how the universe began to how this piece of rock we call earth got where it is. The truth is there are so many things that these scientists do not know, in fact there is a volume of evidence out there showing they are wrong about so many things, it is hard to take them seriously about anything.

Did you know there is an underground city hidden beneath Death Valley, California? These ruins could be as much as five thousand years old. Have you heard about America's ancient "mysteries stone" found by a couple of construction workers in 1872? Were you taught in school about the discovery of the "Judaculla Rock," or the discovery and deciphering of the "Back Creek Stone"? How about America's mysterious "Waffle Rock" located in West Virginia? All of these are real, and I bet you never heard about many of them. Some scientists are a lot like politicians they don't ever seem to admit they have ever been wrong, they just die, telling their lies. Not all scientists fall into this category; some of the finest Christian people I have had the honor to know are scientists—amazingly, a couple even still believe in evolution.

As a long-time educator, it seems shameful to me that so few of the physical mysteries of this planet are explored in the classrooms of America. It pains me that so few students have heard about things like the Blythe Intaglios in eastern California, which is similar to the famous Nazca Lines mentioned earlier and exists just a few miles from where I live. We don't teach our students about the massive amount of Hebrew writing on areas above all the major rivers in the eastern half of North America. Few have heard about the mysterious Pedro Mountain Mummy, discovered in 1932 about sixty miles southwest of Casper, Wyoming. Students are unaware of the Great Serpent Mound of Adams County, Ohio, which is considered the most famous ancient earthworks in all North America and is one of the most impressive archaeological remnants of the entire ancient world. Yet this is perhaps the first you have ever heard of it. Why do you think that is?

CHAPTER 5

Flying Saucers (UFOs)

The subject of flying saucers is so wide and broad there have been thousands of books written on the subject. I intend to give only a modest overview of UFOs in Russia and the former Soviet Union and also review a few major UFO stories from the United States. UFO sightings are so widespread that it's difficult to talk to anyone that hasn't had an unexplained sighting themselves or knows someone who has had a UFO sighting. California seems to be the number one state for UFO sightings, reporting 490 in 2017. Florida was second with 308 reports, followed by Washington with 192 reports, Arizona had 180 reports, and New York had 170 reports of UFO sightings. New Mexico, home of Roswell the site of the famous 1947 UFO incident, came in with 73 reported sightings for 2017. The state with the fewest reported sightings in 2017 was North Dakota with only six reported sightings. The National UFO Reporting Center (NUFORC), the organization that curates reports of UFO sightings in the United States and Canada, has operated almost continuously since 1974. The organization logged a total of 4,655 sightings in 2017, which was unusually down from 2016 which had a total of 5619 sightings.

According to UFORC, on December 14, 2017, a woman reported that she and her husband saw a triangular object with bright green lights near Santa Fe, New Mexico. According to the UFORC report she said they saw the object fly across the interstate in a south easterly direction, and the woman, who wished to remain anonymous, stated,

> *My husband and I were driving northeast on I-25 between Albuquerque and Santa Fe at around 7 p.m. (19:00) on Thursday, December 14, 2017. Suddenly, at around the Waldo Canyon exit, we saw an object flying across the Interstate in a southeasterly direction. It appeared triangular with bright green lights around its entire periphery. From my husband's perspective, it appeared larger than a full moon. By the time it crossed my field of vision (I was in the passenger seat), it appeared slightly smaller than a full moon. It was perhaps several hundred feet in front and above us and appeared to be moving at about 100 mph or less. It seemed to be heading down and then it vanished.*

Reports such as this one are made daily in this country, but until recently, no one really knew what was going on in Russia and the old Soviet Union. Soviet Russia was a very restrictive regime and everything that happened, including UFO sightings, stayed secret within the Russian government or there were terrible consequences. The Soviet Union kept secrets from everybody, the West, as well as their own people. When the Soviet Union was dissolved so was the national security agency called the KGB, and at that time many KGB files fell into the hands of former agents. Thousands of files were smuggled out of the former Soviet Union by people who had worked for the KGB from 1972 until 1984. One of the topics of files smuggled out of the Soviet Union was UFOs, and UFO encounters. After the fall of the Soviet Union and the KGB, many of the thousands of smuggled files concerning UFOs and UFO encounters were made public and are still gradually coming to the light of day. ANCIENT ASTRONAUT THEORISTS say that Soviet records have been covering up the fact that the Soviet Union had been visited by extraterrestrials for years and was also covering up the fact that our planet was visited by extraterrestrials far in the distant past.

Dr. Genrikh Mavrikiyevich Ludvig was imprisoned in one of Stalin's brutal labor camps, but in 2011, thirty years after his death, in an article in a top Russian newspaper (Sovershenno Sekretno) the true purpose of Dr. Ludvig's work was revealed, which also could have been the reason for his imprisonment. Ludvig visited the Vatican around the age of twenty and claimed he was able to look at restricted parts of the Vatican library. There he said, he discovered several manuscripts that suggested there had been recorded extraterrestrial contact with ancient civilizations in Egypt, Israel, and Mesopotamia. These papers described energy machines related to the pyramids.

In 1917, the Soviet state eliminated all types of personal religion. Newly revealed files indicate that a highly secret state religion believed that human civilization had origins in outer space and believed our destiny as human beings was to move back into space; where we would then return into the cradle of civilization. After Stalin died many of those individuals exploring this ancient philosophy were allowed to voice their opinion publicly. Several noted psychologists and mathematicians published papers proposing that extraterrestrials had visited ancient civilizations in ancient times.

Russia has the largest land mass of any country on earth, 50 percent of Russia is uninhabitable and largely unexplored by mankind. To give you an idea of the enormous size of Russia, the United States expands over four-time zones while Russia expands over eleven separate time zones. Much of Russia has a very harsh climate, which makes it very difficult to explore. Many sites in Russia seem to have been used in ancient times for some type of operations, ANCIENT ASTRONAUT THEORISTS claim that these sites may have been take-off points for space ships in ancient times. A large amount of data that included information from Russian pilots was published 1968, and it revealed hundreds of UFO cases from all over the Soviet Union. Some spoke of ships that were small, and others spoke of spacecraft that were very large, some spherical, some cigar-shaped. They reported that these UFOs achieved incredible speeds that no human could survive. Several records from the Soviet Air Force and the KGB date back to the fifties, sixties, and seventies. These reports took the subject of UFO sightings very seriously.

Throughout the 1960s and most of the 1970s, the Soviet government's interest in UFOs remained unofficial. But that changed after September 20, 1977, when numerous residents reported seeing a glowing object floating in the sky for over five minutes showering their city with rays of light. Similar sightings were reported from all across Russia and Eastern Europe within a four-hour window of the first sighting.

Major General Pavel Romanovich Popovich, the eighth man to ever go into space, also has some interesting views on UFOs and extraterrestrials. He had a significant sighting in 1978, when he was flying back from the United States to Russia, and he and several others on a commercial flight saw a triangular craft moving much faster than the airliner they were aboard. Popovich has also stated that the Soviet government knows of three underwater bases currently being inhabited and operated by extraterrestrials.

Marina Popovich's (no relation to Major General Pavel Romanovich Popovich) childhood was marked by Nazi violence and she later explained that her decision to become a pilot was forged out of the need for vengeance. Popovich was a military test pilot by 1964 and during her career tested more than fifty airplanes and broke over one hundred aviation world endurance records, including the longest flight ever by a female pilot. She was the first women to break the sound barrier and she was decorated dozens of times over. Colonel Popovich showed photographs of cigar-shaped crafts at a press conference in San Francisco in 1990. In her 2003 book, *UFO Glasnost*, Popovich states that over three thousand UFO sightings have been made by military and civilian pilots from the USSR. She claimed that the USSR was in possession of fragments from five different crashed UFOs and claimed to have seen photographs that were in the possession of Soviet officials that showed alien/human highbred children. Marina Popovich died on November 30, 2017, at the age of eighty-six.

The event that has come to be known as the "Russian Roswell," occurred in 1986 when several hundred witnesses saw a UFO crash into a Russian mountain range. Material was recovered from the crash site, which yielded unusual results, the remains contained complex systems of woven fibers with an atomic structure that caused the material itself to change when it was exposed to heat. Anonymous sources stated that some of the materials seem to be some kind of machinery that was not of this earth and a number of Russian scientists stated that they had seen technology that does not exist on earth today. That area has reported many UFO sightings sense the crash, and ANCIENT ASTRONAUT THEORISTS believe that Russians have had contact with extraterrestrials here on earth as well as in space.

Russian cosmonauts aboard the Russian Scientific Research Space Station have reported many strange sightings involving floating orange glowing gases that move around and then engulf the entire station. Then suddenly as the glowing orange cloud collapsed, they were all blinded by the orange light. When they regained their vision, they looked out the portals of the space station and were astonished at the site of seven angelic beings that were traveling alongside their spacecraft. The angelic beings stayed with the space station for over ten minutes, the cosmonauts described them as huge winged creatures, some as much is eighty feet tall with glowing halos. Officials dismissed the incident as a group hallucination resulting from oxygen deprivation and pressure fluctuations in the space station. Later that year in the summer, three more cosmonauts join the crew of three already living in the space station. All six cosmonauts later reported once again seeing the winged angelic beings accompanying the space station from a distance.

The question is could these really be angels, angelic beings from another dimension? There are audio recordings from another event that took place between two cosmonauts while they were in orbit in the late 1990s, and they heard voices. There is a conversation that took place and somehow someone or something was speaking to the cosmonauts in a foreign language. According to one of the cosmonauts, the voices were distant and undistinguishable, but both said it was inside their heads and seemed like a telepathic message being sent to them. They felt it was a cosmic whisper that was coming from their ancestors, from a very distant past, and it told them about things concerning their own family in Russia that no one could have ever known. The angelic beings also told them that they should go back to earth, and that Russia was not ready for what they were attempting to do in space.

Reportedly, in the United States, UFO sightings are much more prevalent in states that are close to water. Many believe aliens are living below the frozen oceans on ours and other planets, and they believe the most inhabitable planets for extraterrestrials are ones completely covered with water. Some believers in extraterrestrials think that some of the flying saucers we see are nothing more than aliens out house hunting for a new planet that can sustain life. Some also believe that these aliens live in extraterrestrial cities at the bottom of our oceans. ANCIENT ASTRONAUT THEORISTS believe that extraterrestrials living at the bottom of our oceans come and go with frequency. With that in mind, it seems ironic that the most famous of all US UFO sightings took place in the New Mexico desert.

On July 8, 1947, perhaps the most famous UFO incident in US history occurred. According to the United States Air Force this incident involved a United States Army Air Force balloon that crashed at a ranch near Roswell, New Mexico. Officials from the airfield at Roswell originally announced it had recovered a "flying disc," but later reports from the US military said it was merely a conventional weather balloon. Interest in the incident was revived in the late 1970s when UFO investigators claimed that an extraterrestrial spacecraft crashed near the Roswell Army air base, and that the US military had engaged in a cover-up of the incident. Later, in the 1990s, two reports were published by the US military, and in these reports the secrecy surrounding Roswell was explained by claiming the nature of the crash object was actually a nuclear test surveillance balloon from project Mogul. Project Mogul was a top-secret project run by the US Army Air Forces which involved microphones attached to high-altitude balloons that would detect the sound waves generated by Soviet atomic bomb testing. Although Roswell is considered by many government experts, to be the most thoroughly investigated and totally debunked UFO claim in US history, questions and disbelievers remain.

William Brazel, a ranch foreman in the area was first to notice clusters of debris scattered on the ground about thirty miles north of Roswell, New Mexico. The description and photographs of the debris field discovered by Brazel do not seem to support the theory that this was some type of rubber balloon. Confusing the issue even more, on July 8, 1947, the Airfield Public Information Officer, Walter Haut issued a press release stating that the 509's Operation Group had recovered a flying disc which had crashed on a ranch near Roswell, New Mexico. For over sixty years, there have been books, articles, movies, and TV specials based on the 1947 Roswell incident. By 1997, when CNN/Time conducted a poll on people's beliefs about aliens and Roswell, many people interviewed for the poll believed that aliens had visited Earth and landed at Roswell, and that the incident had been covered up by the United States government. It would be my guess that now twenty years later, the results of a similar poll would show that even more people believed that aliens have visited Earth and landed at Roswell.

Perhaps you have seen the movie *Fire in the Sky*, a 1993 Paramount production, or read the book by Travis Walton. It was based on actual events which reportedly took place in the White Mountains of Arizona, on November 5, 1975. Travis Walton, a member of a seven-man tree trimming team, was struck down by a luminous blue light coming from a UFO and then disappeared for five days. According to Walton's book, after a full day's work the seven-man team witnessed a bright light coming through the trees as they were traveling home on a logging road. As they came closer to the light, they saw a golden disk hovering about ninety feet above the ground. Walton jumped from the truck and ran toward the craft; he was struck down by a blue-green bolt coming from the bottom of the spacecraft. The rest of the crew watched in shock as their buddy laid motionless on the ground, then fearing for their own lives drove off as fast as they could. As the fear wore off, the driver of the truck decided they had to go back for Walton and turned around. When they reached the area where the incident took place, they could find no signs of a struggle or of Walton.

The incident was reported to the Navajo County Sheriff's office, and a search for Walton was started, which continued for four days. As the search continued, the six men who witnessed the event volunteered to take polygraph tests at the local courthouse, and all passed the test with positive readings. Five days after his disappearance, on November 10, Walton, confused, shaken, and bewildered, found himself alongside the highway about one half a mile west of the town of Heber, Arizona. After calling his sister from a nearby phone booth, Walton was picked up by his brother and brother-in-law. While Walton was dehydrated, had lost about ten pounds, and was suffering from malnutrition, he didn't appear to have any physical injuries. Walton was examined by reputable medical doctors and psychologists, and under regressive hypnosis, he related seeing frightening alien beings of two different kinds, who never communicated with him but seemed to be very interested in his physical anatomy. Walton was also given a polygraph and voice stress test, which he passed with a positive rating indicating he was telling the truth and was mentally stable. Now sixty years later, the White Mountain incident has never been debunked or explained to the satisfaction of investigators that have looked at the case.

On December 26, 2017, a report made by United States Air Force personnel, was released to the public. The report tells of the sighting of an unidentified object, which was trailing their aircraft across the Atlantic Ocean. According to reports, the aircraft was originally traveling from Charleston Air Force Base, South Carolina to Dover Air Force Base, Delaware, when the UFO was picked up on their radar, and was pacing their aircraft. The crew reported the incident to the tower once they landed at Dover, and technicians checked their radar but found no problem. The report continues; the plane then took off from Dover in route to Ireland, but halfway across the Atlantic Ocean, the same object appeared and continued to follow them the rest of the way across the Atlantic. The report states that the aircraft again contacted the tower to report the encounter, and the tower reported that they had the object on their radar as well. As happens too often, the crew decided not to file a UFO report because they feared it would be bad for their careers. A recording of the actual radar image has been released and shown widely on US television.

This latest sighting by United States Air Force personnel comes on the heels of the recent comments by former astronaut Buzz Aldrin, about the mysterious monolith discovered on Phobos, one of Mar's two moons. Reportedly, the Mars monolith is a rectangle object, some say a boulder, photographed by the Mars Reconnaissance Orbiter, and was first observed in 1998. Recently it has been reported that Aldrin, the second man to walk on the moon, stated that the monolith on Phobos is a very unusual structure and that when people find out about it they're going to be asking some serious questions. Like, who put it there?

There are far too many UFO sightings daily, to do anything but scratch the surface when discussing this subject here. What I hope I've done, is provide you with a feeling of how large and widespread the body of evidence is supporting claims that something strange and unnatural is going on in our skies. Many sightings, I believe, are easily explained, but I personally have seen things in the night sky, over the Colorado River that are in my mind, totally unexplainable.

Other sightings seem to have reasonable explanations that can be easily believed. I remember an evening, back in the 1980s when I was in the parking lot of a local convenience store around closing time. Suddenly, out of the southwestern sky, over the hills west of the Colorado River, came a large fiery ball the likes of which I had never seen before. The ball of fire looked larger than a normal full moon, and the noise that accompanied the fire ball sounded like when you shake up a bottle of soda pop and then slowly release the build up from inside the bottle. As the ball of fire from the southwest moved eastward, I stood in the parking lot watching the huge fire ball pass over my head rushing toward Phoenix. I was in a state of shock! I had no idea how high in the night sky this fiery ball of fire was, but to my untrained eye it seemed to be maybe only five hundred to one thousand feet above my head. The things that raced through my mind were horrifying, I envisioned everything from a nuclear attack to a "life as we know it" ending asteroid about to meet earth.

Stunned but energized by survival adrenalin, I rushed home to check the Phoenix television news. It was not long before reports came pouring in, thousands of people saw the fiery ball and reported it to police, news organizations, and television stations all over Arizona. The reports said that it was a Russian satellite reentering our atmosphere and had crashed somewhere west of Phoenix in the middle of the Arizona desert. This meant my height estimates were way off and the ball of fire must have been way larger than it appeared. I believed the reports at the time, and I believe them to this day, I have no reason not to. There will always be skeptics, and many would insist that it must have been something more than an old used up Russian satellite entering the atmosphere. I admit it was an amazing sight, but my point is; sometimes there are reasonably simple answers for some of the things we see in the sky, and sometimes there are not.

PART TWO

ANGELS

CHAPTER 6

Pyramid of Giza and Monoliths in the Bible

I think there is more than enough physical evidence existing on this planet from ancient civilizations that were here thousands of years before accepted history acknowledges the existence of any civilization, to convince anyone this is real. One of these anomalies existing in our world should be enough to start one wondering about where it may have come from, but with hundreds of examples worldwide, and more being found all the time, we need to wake up to the facts. You can find examples everywhere you look, just start digging. You might want to start your research with the recent discovery of an ancient city with giant carved steps made of stone blocks like those of the Great Pyramid of Giza that is totally submerged under fifty feet of water. Just Google "ancient underwater city found" and you will find plenty of information on it. I need to make one thing perfectly crystal clear; I believe most of the evidence presented by Erich von Daniken and other ANCIENT ASTRONAUT THEORISTS is authentic. Admittedly, they get off on some crazy wild tangents sometimes involving reincarnation, mind control, and other far out stuff, but when you look at the physical evidence they present much of it is just undeniable. For the record, I believe, the biggest problem with the ANCIENT ASTRONAUT THEORISTS is that they use the term extraterrestrial beings instead of the correct term supernatural beings. This one mistake takes them off 180 degrees in the wrong direction. They fail to recognize the truth; that the beings they describe as being extraterrestrial are actually supernatural beings from another dimension, as is described in the Bible.

The first thing we must understand about God, if we are ever going to come to any real understanding of His nature, is that as the Creator of heaven and earth, He is the master mathematician and scientist. Everything that we see here on earth must, by definition, fit into God's Natural Law. If just one time, without any outside assistance, you drop a pencil from your hand and it doesn't fall to the ground, the Law of Gravity will cease to be a Natural Law. So how does this relate to the Great Pyramid of Giza? First, the procedures used to build the Great Pyramid must have adhered to the Laws of Nature. Second, if this was true at the time the Great Pyramid was constructed, there must have been some advanced technology available to allow it to happen. In my opinion, there is no reasonable explanation how the Pyramid of Giza could have been built using only the ancient methods we have been taught were available to the Egyptians of that time. There is no way they could have feed a work force large enough to build the structure, and there is no way they could have moved stones of the size and weight used in its construction with only the ancient methods they had at the time.

The Great Pyramid of Giza is written of in the Bible in more than one place. The most commonly referenced place the Pyramid of Giza is mentioned in the Bible is in Isaiah 19:19–20 where it is speaking of a future time:

> *19 In that day shall there be an altar to the Lord in the midst of the land of Egypt, and a pillar at the border thereof to the Lord.*

> *20 And it shall be for a sign and for a witness unto the Lord of hosts in the land of Egypt: for they shall cry unto the Lord because of the oppressors, and he shall send them a savior and a great one, and he shall deliver them.*

Few Christians fail to see this as a reference to the End Times and the Second Coming of Christ, but some still argue this is not a reference to the Pyramid of Giza. The main argument is over the word pillar and the decenters claim that a pyramid is not a pillar. They refer to other places in the Bible where pillar is used, and in those places, it refers to just that; a pillar. The problem with this argument is that the word translated as pillar in the nineteenth chapter and ninetieth verse of Isaiah is *not* the word they are referring to; which from the Hebrew is Strong's number 5982. The word they refer to is usually translated pillar and almost always means pillar.

However, the word in Isaiah 19 is Strong's number 4676, which can mean a pillar but usually means a monument. In fact, if you look at most other places this word is used and translated pillar in the King James it refers to things such as head stones and other types of monuments to people. One example of the use of this word is in the description of the stone monument Absalom, son of David, erected to himself as is recorded in the Second Book of Samuel. A pillar can be a monument, but all monuments are definitely not pillars. Besides, the verse also states that this monument is going to be an alter to the Lord, which doesn't fit the normal use of a pillar either.

The word *pyramid* is not found in the King James Translation of the Bible, but the word is in the Apocrypha in 1 Maccabees 13:26–28, which correctly refers to them as monuments:

> *26 And all Israel lamented him greatly and mourned over him for a long time.*
>
> *27 And Simon built a monument over the grave of his father and his brothers, and made it high so that it could be seen, with polished stone on back and front.*
>
> *28 And he erected seven pyramids in a row, for his father and his mother and his four brothers.*

The Apocrypha was not canonized in 397 AD with the rest of our Old and New Testament but was included in the original 1611 English translation of the King James Version of the Bible. According to history, most Hebrew scholars considered the Apocrypha to be good historical and religious documents, but not on the same level as the Hebrew Scriptures. So the referral to the pyramids as monuments should be reliable.

It is also obvious in two other verses of the New Testament that Jesus Himself referred to the Great Pyramid of Giza. One of the most striking things about the Great Pyramid is the fact that the top corner stone is missing. Jesus compares the missing corner stone of the Great Pyramid of Giza to the fact that He, the Messiah, will also be missing until His return in the End Times. It states in Mathew 21:42,

> *42 Jesus saith unto them, Did ye never read in the scriptures, the stone which the builders rejected, the same is become the head of the corner: this is the Lord's doing, and it is marvelous in our eyes?*

Paul also refers to Christ as the chief corner stone in Ephesians 2:20, and in Psalm 118:22 we find the verse of which Jesus was speaking:

> *The stone which the builders refused is become the head stone of the corner.*

Remember, this was written in the Old Testament long before the birth of Christ, it must be future prophesy making a reference to a known stone construct of the time. What could it be referring to other than the Great Pyramid of Giza? The burning question that remains for many is, who were the builders? Who really built this amazing structure that's existence alone seems to be a challenge to explain? Why were the stone blocks used in its construction so large, and how were they moved? The cement used to glue the facing stones on the outside surface of the Great Pyramid is so strong we can't duplicate it today. The inside structure of the building is a mystery; the exact measurements of the tunnels and rooms and what they represent are a source of endless discussion and debate. There is evidence that a chemical reaction took place inside the pyramid and there is construction under it that may have been related to the creation of energy. And the very top, the cornerstone is missing. It is evident that the Great Pyramid of Giza was never used for burial as a tomb, so what was the purpose of this amazing building. This unexplainable relic, one of the Seven Ancient Wonders of the World, what could it be other than as a monument?

To understand the physical mysteries, we find on earth we must accept that these physical realities found in the dimension in which we are living, must have been created according to the Laws of Physics. As Bible-believing Christians, we must also accept that God created this dimension and put us in it, also through methods that are governed by His Physical Law. But how do we fit into all of it? In the King James Bible, Jeremiah 32:18–20 reads:

> *18 Thou showest loving kindness onto thousands, and recompensest the iniquity of the fathers into the bosom of their children after them: the Great the Mighty God, the Lord of hosts is his (His) name,*

> *19 Great in counsel, and mighty in work: for thine eyes are open upon all the ways of the sons of men: to give everyone according to his ways, and according to the fruit of his doing:*

Are your eyes opened as well as your ears? Is your heart open to understand? God left the fruit of some of ancient mankind's labor for us to see. Our belief in His wonderous power should be reinforced by the physical existence of these relics; we need to get busy producing fruit.

> *20 Which has set signs and wonders in the land of Egypt, even unto this day, and in Israel, and amongst other men; and hast made thee a name…*

Look around the world today; you have been presented with some amazing physical evidence of what went on in ancient times. I believe verse 20 of Jeremiah 32 is speaking about the Great Pyramid of Giza, and the other giant monoliths of the world left behind for us as signs. Examining these physical signs, we must accept the fact that many of these relics of the past, relics from ancient times were produced by unexplained technology for unexplained reasons. I believe, we must also accept the possibility that God Himself, with the help of His angels was the main architect and builder of them. ANCIENT ASTRONAUT THEORISTS leap to the conclusion that these mystifying objects must involve some type of extraterrestrial race from outer space that is as yet undiscovered. As a Christian, it seems more sensible to accept the premise presented in the Bible that these things were done by supernatural beings from another dimension, which we call heaven or paradise.

CHAPTER 7

Parable of the Tares

Let's continue on the subject of how we fit into all this. Note the use of the word *fathers* in Jeremiah 32:18, on the surface this seems to be talking about the evil fathers of the evil children of the world. But did you know in a spiritual and physical sense Christ said there are two fathers, and there are two sets of children that follow them? Jesus spoke of it several times pointing out to the Pharisees that they followed their fathers who killed the prophets and were of their father the first murderer. So the first of the two fathers, whose children are the evil ones of the world was the first murderer. We all know the first murderer was Cain, then Jesus went on to tell the Pharisees that if they had been of His Father they would believe and love Him. This goes all the way back to the garden and what happened there. Jesus set it straight for us and revealed the truth, when he explained the Parable of the Tares of the Field, in Matthew 13:36–43. Remember, the disciples came to Jesus and told Him they didn't understand the parable He had just taught. Let's lay a little ground work and read the following with understanding.

> *36 Then Jesus sent the multitude away and went into the house: and his disciples came unto him, saying, Declare unto us the parable of the tares of the field.* (Mathew 13:36)

Christ's disciples didn't understand the Parable of the Tares of the Field, which you can find earlier in Matthew 13:24–30. They wanted Jesus to explain it to them.

> *37 He answered and said unto them, He that soweth the good seed is the Son of man;*

So again, this is not a parable, it is Christ explaining the parable. Christ is saying the person who is sowing the good seed is God, Jesus Christ.

> *38 The field is the world; the good seed are the children of the kingdom; but the tares are the children of the wicked one;*

> *39 The enemy that sowed them is the devil; the harvest is the end of the world; and the reapers are the angels.*

So there are physical children in this physical world that were God's; the children of Adam. And there are physical children in this physical world that were the Devil's; the children of Cain. The thing you need to understand about tares is that it is a weed, and it looks just like wheat when the plants are young. As they grow more mature you can see the difference between the two. Do not think this is a "spiritual father child relationship," the word *seed* in the Greek is number 4690 in the Strong's: sperma—something sown including male sperm. Jesus says the harvest is the end of this earth-age and because we will be in our spiritual bodies by that time, angels will be doing the work.

> *40 As therefore the tares are gathered and burnt in the fire; so, shall it be in the end of this world.*

> *41 The Son of man shall send forth his angels, and they shall gather out of his kingdom all things that offend, and them which do iniquity;*

42 And shall cast them into a furnace of fire: there shall be wailing and gnashing of teeth.

43 Then shall the righteous shine forth as the sun in the kingdom of their Father. Who hath ears to hear, let him hear.

Can you hear the truth? Do you know which father you are following? I hope so, only one will get you into the Kingdom.

When we talk about different dimensions, many Christians roll their eyes and think it's crazy talk. Seems ironic to me that the atheistic leaning ANCIENT ASTRONAUT THEORISTS are more willing to accept the idea of different dimensions than God-fearing Christians. The truth is, different dimensions is exactly what the Bible teaches, from the very beginning of the Old Testament, in Genesis 1:26 God says to His host;

And God said, Let us make man in our image, after our likeness: and let them have dominion over the fish of the sea, and over the fowl of the air, and over the cattle, and over all the earth, and over every creeping thing that creepeth upon the earth.

I hope you understand the things God gave man dominion over are here on earth in this dimension of the flesh. Think about it, if we are here on earth in the flesh and we die, where does the soul go? The Bible says it returns to the Father, God the Father, not the other father. I also hope you don't believe God the Father is in the flesh, or that He normally lives in the dimension of the flesh! So how can there not be different dimensions and travel between them, spiritual travel as well as physical travel? Is it beyond imagination because this universe is so vast that earth would be the only planet that supports intelligent life? That is one of the arguments ANCIENT ASTRONAUT THEORISTS put forth supporting their belief extraterrestrial aliens must exist on other planets. What if the entire universe is being used, only it is being used in another dimension we cannot see?

So who was God's host whom He called *us* in Genesis 1:26 and where was this host located? God explained it all in the letter He wrote us. God tells us the story in several places in the Bible; how Satan tried to overthrow God and a multitude of God's souls followed Satan. When Satan was defeated, rather than destroying those souls that followed Satan, God commanded all souls, His host, to be born into the dimension of flesh, to choose once and for all between good and evil. Can you imagine being put in a position where you would have to choose to destroy one of your own children? That's the decision God faced when Satan tried to overthrow Him, but it involved thousands upon thousands, probably millions upon millions of His children.

In the twenty-eighth chapter of Ezekiel, God gives us a great picture of Satan and how because of pride he tried to replace God. Satan had everything, he was a cherub, he was beautiful, and he was powerful. Satan was wise and in Revelation 12:4, we are told that he was able to deceive a third of God's souls who followed him in his rebellion. God chose not to destroy his children, but brought on the Second Earth and Heaven Age, as is described in Second Peter to allow His souls a chance to redeem themselves.

So the host is all of God's souls, and after Satan's rebellion each of God's souls were required to be born into the Second Earth Age, in flesh bodies, here on earth, without knowledge of the First Earth Age. The earth had been inhabited previously, before God created mankind in the flesh, by supernatural beings. We are told this in the Bible, and we see evidence of the existence of these beings all over the globe today. We, God's souls, were here before in our spiritual bodies living in a different dimension. Have you ever wondered why, continuing in the first chapter of Genesis in verse 28, God blessed His creation; mankind in flesh bodies and ordered them to be fruitful, to multiply, and to *replenish* the earth? Have you ever tried to replenish a brand-new anything? A brand-new refrigerator? A brand-new chest of drawers? A brand-new gas-tank? It is impossible! To replenish anything, it must have been used and have been filled in the past.

Consider Jesus Christ for a moment, when He returned to His disciples after the crucifixion, as it is described in the Gospels. Jesus didn't open the door and walk in, He walked through the wall. He was of a different dimension; His body had been transfigured. But wait a minute, while Jesus, in His transfigured body, walked through the wall, Timothy was able to put his finger in the Lord's wounds and feel His body. How can that be you might ask? Well, obviously one does not exclude the other, the spiritual body has mass too, but it is different. In fact, we have several examples in the New and Old Testament of how supernatural bodies have mass and in some ways function in the same way human bodies do. For example, and we will be talking more about them later, but we are told in the Bible that the sons of God (Fallen Angels) came to earth and mated with the daughters of Adam and had offspring. We are also told in Exodus that during the forty years Israel wandered in the desert, God fed them with manna, which is by definition angel food. So angels eat, they have the ability to reproduce with humans in this earth age, and yet they still come from a different dimension and have spiritual bodies. This is what the Word of God tells us.

If you are still having a problem with the idea of different dimensions, and the life that exists in each dimension, consider God Himself. The Bible teaches us that God's Spirit entered a human form, whom we call Jesus Christ, and He became Emmanuel, which simply means "God with us" in Hebrew. Think about that for a minute; God would never ask us to do anything He wouldn't do Himself, so he too was born into the flesh. Just as His host was required to be born into the flesh, He allowed Himself to be born into this world of flesh, to live and die here on earth.

This is the appropriate time and place to address Erich von Daniken's question I referred to earlier; why would God need a vehicle if He is supernatural? His question is of course based on the "idea" that God is all-powerful and can do anything He wants, but the truth is a little more complicated. There are some things that God can't or won't do, God can't make you love Him, because then it wouldn't be true love. Similarly, God won't violate his own Natural Laws any more than He would let us violate them. Once God violated His own Law it wouldn't be a law any longer. Even a "Sunday Scientist," as von Daniken describes himself, should recognize that in science a law is a law is a law. I used to have fun with my students, when I would ask the class if they knew the difference between a law and a theory. Of course they did and we would all come to agreement that a theory is only an idea of what might or might not happened, while a law is absolute. The example I gave before of gravity being a Law of Nature will do nicely. Again, if just once you drop that pencil and it doesn't fall to the ground then the Law of Gravity becomes the Theory of Gravity. Then I would ask the students if certain things were laws or theories. You might want to play along:

"Is Evolution a theory or a law?"

"Is Global Warming a theory or a law?"

"Is Christianity a theory or a law?"

"Is Natural Selection a theory or a law?"

"Is 'Extraterrestrial Sperminazation of Humans' a theory or a law?"

The answer to all these questions is the same: they are all theories, and none of them can be proven so they all must be believed on faith to some degree or another.

Let's get back to von Daniken's question. Why in the world would God need a vehicle? It seems obvious to me if you are transporting anything with mass, according to Natural Law you would need something with which to transport it, especially if it was between different dimensions. God not only had His supernatural body onboard that vehicle, but He had his physical throne upon which He sat when He spoke to Moses.

> *"We are natural, God is supernatural, that just means He's more natural than we are."* (Arnold Murray, 1983)

CHAPTER 8

The Overthrow

Biblically speaking, to have any chance to truly understand what's going on in the world today, as well as what will happen tomorrow, we must understand what happened in the beginning. It's puzzling to me, how there can be so many Christians living day to day that have no real concrete idea of how they got here. Millions upon millions of our Christian brothers and sisters not only don't know where they came from but don't know why they are here, or what God expects of them. For us to understand what happened in the beginning, we need to start at Genesis 1:1. To check me out, you are going to need a King James Version of the Bible, and a Strong's Exhaustive Concordance of the Bible, preferably a Hendrickson edition as old as you can find.

Confusion abounds and in these End Times we must be careful to choose the correct tools for our research. The reason it's important to use a King James Version of the Bible rather than some of the newer translations, is that we have the Strong's Exhaustive Concordance of the Bible, which allows us to take any word in the King James back to the original language in which it was written and see what that word meant in its original language. This is very important to remember: there are evil forces in the world that are trying to promote the agenda of Satan himself. Evidence of this can be readily found in not only some new translations of the Bible, but also in some new editions of James Strong's work.

James Strong, STD, LLD, spent much of his life working on his epic project, which was finally published in the late 1800s. The Word of God was set in stone, each word with its original meanings. Now, in the twenty-first century, we find modern editions of James Strong's work published with glaring erroneous changes and additions to his work. My overall message to you, my Christian brother and sister, is be careful, this is the time of great deception, described in Matthew 24:4 and thereafter. There is no other reasonable explanation for the changes that have been made in new translations of the Bible and editions of James Strong's work, other than that the forces of evil are trying to mislead God's children.

Let's start right at the beginning; the first thing God wants us to know is in Genesis 1:1:

> *In the beginning God created the heaven and the earth.*

Do you understand what that verse states? It says that in the very beginning God created the heaven and the earth—period. The "period" at the end of that sentence means this is the end of that thought. Then, there is a second thought presented in the second and third sentence of the Bible, it states:

> *And the earth was without form, and void; and darkness was upon the face of the deep. And the Spirit of God moved upon the face of the waters.* (Genesis 1:2)

So God created the heaven and the earth in the first verse and destroyed the earth in the second. Between the end of the first sentence and the beginning of the next sentence the entire First Earth Age, which is described in Second Peter as well as other places, took place.

There is an enormous problem with this translation, if you check out the word *was* used in both places in that verse, it is word number 1961 in the Strong's, if you look it up you will find that word means *became.* So let's read the verse with understanding as it was written in:

> *And the earth became void and without form, and*
> *darkness became the face of the deep. And the Spirit*
> *of God moved upon the face of the waters.*

Quite a difference! If you use the translation "was" you are led to believe that God created earth void in the beginning. But when correctly translating the Hebrew word, which is Strong's number 1961 *"hayah,"* which is a prime root word in Hebrew, it means: *to become, or come to pass.* We are clearly shown that at some point in time this beautiful creation of God's (earth), became void and without form. Isaiah 45:18 is a second witness of what state in which the earth was created:

> *For thus saith the Lord that created the heavens;*
> *God himself that formed the earth and made it; he*
> *hath established it. He created it not in vain, he*
> *formed it to be inhabited: I am the Lord; and there*
> *is none else.*

So God created the heavens and the earth and they were beautiful and were inhabited for a whole earth age. The word *vain* is the same word that is also translate *without form* in Genesis 1:2, and Isaiah tells us this is not what earth was like in the beginning. In other words, earth was created and established and supported life from its beginning. Then, after an entire earth age something happened and God destroyed the earth, and in Genesis 1:2 we are told it was destroyed by water.

The fact that a gigantic flood, at some time in the past, covered the entire landmass on earth should not be in dispute. From fossil records, to ancient accounts in almost every civilization a devastating catastrophic flood is recorded. There are many theories on what might have caused this catastrophic flood, but there is little doubt that it took place several thousand years ago. Where I live in Arizona, you can see in many places, such as at highway and railroad construction, where different layers of the earth have been exposed and you can see seashells and other fossil remains of sea life. It's obvious that the ocean once covered this landmass; the same is true across the globe. This is the point where most biblically illiterate Christians go wrong.

"Oh yeah, I know all about the flood, Noah and all the animals…" they will say. No, sorry. Wrong flood. You didn't know there were two floods? Well let's compare the two, and you can make up your own mind.

The first flood as is reported in the second verse, of the first chapter of Genesis is described as *had no form* and *was void*. Let's examine these words. The first word translated *without form* in your Strong's, is number *8414 "tohuw"; to lie waste; a desolation; in vain, confusion, empty place, without form, nothing.* The second word, translated *"void"* in your Strong's, is number *922 "bohuw"; to be empty; a vacuity; a distinguishable ruin: emptiness, void.* When you link these two words together, as they are in the second verse of Genesis:

"without form, and void…"

It has double emphasis! What power! Is there any question in your mind that every living thing was destroyed in this flood? It is so emphatic, there should be no doubt.

Now let's look at the second flood, Noah's flood. I'm going to tread on to some dangerous ground with some denominations of Christianity with this, but what's new? I'm going to propose to you the possibility that Noah's flood was not worldwide. There are things that survived his flood, such as the descendants of Cain, better known as Kenites. Their existence after Noah's flood is undeniable (Genius 15:19, Numbers 24:21, Judges 4:11, 1 Samuel 15:6, Chronicles 2:55, and others). Their existence is difficult to explain unless you believe Noah took two of all the races onto the Ark, and if you hold that belief you then must explain how two of all the races were collected by Noah from all the different corners of the globe. Most clear-thinking Christians should agree that Noah could only bring on to his Ark those animals and humans, living in his nearby vicinity. Some will say, "There weren't any other races on earth at the time." Really? Where did the races come from then? These people need to go back to Genesis 1:27 and 28; God created males and females and told them to go replenish the earth. This was before God rested on the seventh day and before He *formed* Adam and Eve (Genesis 2:7).

At the same time, when you look at a map of what is believed to have been Noah's neighborhood, it is in an area surrounded by mountains, which include the Andes. The area forms a natural basin, and some believe that it was this area only that was flooded. There are stories in several Ancient Eastern Civilizations of a great flood that took place on the other side of their mountains (the Andes). Either way, we know certain things survived Noah's flood, and from the definitions of *"without form"* and *"void"* in the Hebrew language it is impossible for them to refer to a flood where any life survived. I would argue the use of *"without form"* and *"void"* in the verse precludes the possibility of Noah and his family surviving this flood.

Furthermore, in the seventh chapter of Genesis, God tells us the story of what happened to Noah and his descendants, when the rain started falling. It rained forty days and forty nights, and as the water fell, the Ark was raised and lifted from the ground. The Bible then tells us of the destruction that took place on the land where the water fell, and that the water prevailed upon the earth for 150 days. Then in the eighth chapter of Genesis, we are told that Noah opened the window of the ark and sent forth a raven and a dove to see if the waters had resided. Seven days later, Noah sent another dove out from the Ark which returned to him in the evening carrying an olive leaf, from a living olive tree. Does that sound like *"tohuw bohuw"* to you? I don't think so. If everything on earth was killed except the life on Noah's Ark, how did an olive tree that could produce a living leaf survive?

We cannot overlook the reason for Noah's flood and compare it to the flood of Genesis 1:2. The flood of Genesis 1:2 was brought on by Satan's rebellion and the attempted overthrow of God, and the destruction that took place at that time was total.

I beheld the earth, and lo it was without form,
and void; and the heavens, and they had no light.

I beheld the mountains, and lo they trembled, and all the hills moved lightly. I beheld, and lo there was no man, and all the birds of the heavens were fled. I beheld, and lo the fruitful place was a wilderness, and all the cities thereof were broken down at the presence of the Lord, and by his fierce anger. (Jeremiah 4:23–26)

Yes, there were *cities* there, cities of old, and God destroyed them at the overthrow, the ruins of which are still around today. The same event is described in 2 Peter 3:5–7:

For this they willingly are ignorant of, that by the word of God the heavens were of old, and the earth standing out of the water and in the water: whereby the world that then was, being overflowed with water, perished: but the heavens and the earth, which are now, by the same word are kept in store, reserved unto fire against the day of judgment and perdition of ungodly men.

What about the phrase *were of old*, it is an interesting truth that is referred to several times by Paul. When Paul talks about a time long ago, he uses the word *foundation*, as in Ephesians chapter 1 where the subject is the choosing of God's elect:

3 Blessed be the God and Father of our Lord Jesus Christ, who hath blessed us with all spiritual blessings in heavenly places in Christ:

4 According as He hath chosen us in Him before the foundation of the world, that we should be holy and without blame before Him in love.

The word *foundation* in this verse is *"katabole"* Strong's number 2602, from the word *"katabollo"* number 2598 in your Strong's; *to throw down; to cast down.* So it refers back to the casting down at the attempted overthrow by Satan. Let's look at some other places the term *foundation of the world* is used.

In Mathew 13, the disciple is explaining how Jesus always taught in parables:

> *35 That it might be fulfilled which was spoken by the prophet, saying, I will open my mouth in parables; I will utter things which have been kept secret from the foundation of the world.*

In Hebrews chapter 4, Paul is again speaking of the elect and how their works from the first earth age got them to where they are now:

> *3 For we which have believed do enter into rest, as he said, As I have sworn in my wrath, if they shall enter into my rest: although the works were finished from the foundation of the world.*

In Revelation chapter 17, the overthrow and the foundation of the world is spoken of by an angel when John is told the scarlet colored beast in his vision, carrying the woman in Revelation 17:3 is no other than Satan:

> *8 The beast that thou sawest was, and is not; and shall ascend out of the bottomless pit, and go into perdition; and they that dwell on the earth shall wonder, whose names are not written in the book of life, from the foundation of the world when, they behold the beast that was, and is not, and yet is.*

John is speaking of those souls that followed Satan in his rebellion during the First Earth Age and therefore their names are not found in the Book of Life. Satan was here on earth and then banished to heaven when Jesus told him to get behind Him after Satan had tried to tempt Christ. But he is coming back; *the beast that was, and is not, and yet is.* Also, if you have any doubt that verse 8 is referring to Satan and the bottomless pit reference isn't enough; the word *perdition* is Strong's number 684 and in the Greek, it means *destruction, to die, to perish.* There is only one entity in the Bible that has already been condemned, by name, to eternal death by God that would be Satan.

So the First Earth Age was destroyed because of Satan, and God created this Second Earth Age which will be around until the second coming of Christ. But why was God so angry and determined to destroy the First Earth Age? Again, just as Jesus told us in the Book of Matthew, He has told us all things: Isaiah 14:12–17 states,

12 How art thou fallen from heaven, O Lucifer, son of the morning! How art thou cut down to the ground, which didst weaken the nations!

13 For thou hast said in thine heart, I will ascend into heaven, I will exalt my throne above the stars of God: I will sit also upon the mount of the congregation, in the sides of the north:

14 I will ascend above the heights of the clouds; I will be like the most High.

15 Yet thou shalt be brought down to hell, to the sides of the pit.

16 They that see thee shall narrowly look upon thee, and consider thee, saying, Is this the man that made the earth to tremble, that did shake kingdoms;

17 That made the world as a wilderness, and destroyed the cities thereof; that open not the house of his prisoners?

If you have eyes to see and ears to hear, there should be little doubt in your mind at this point, about which event this verse is speaking, and why it took place.

In the second verse of the twenty-eighth chapter of the book of Ezekiel, one of Satan's many names is revealed to us, and once again we are given the why:

> *2 Son of man, say unto the Prince of Tyrus, thus saith the Lord God; because thine heart is lifted up, and thou hast said, I am a God, I sit in the seat of God, in the midst of the seas; yet thou art a man, and not God, though thou set thine heart as the heart of God:*

But what about Noah's flood, what does the word of God tell us was the reason for this flood. In the sixth chapter of Genesis we are told,

> *1 And it came to pass, when men began to multiply on the face of the earth, and daughters were born unto them,*
>
> *2 That the sons of God saw the daughters of men that they were fair; and they took them wives of all which they chose.*
>
> *3 And the Lord said, My spirit shall not always strive with man, for that he also is flesh: yet his days shall be 120 years.*
>
> *4 There were giants in the earth in those days; and also after that, when the sons of God came in unto the daughters of men, and they bear children to them, the same became mighty men which were of old, men of renown.*

The story here is clear and simple, mankind began to multiply, and the *sons of God* were attracted to the female offspring of man. But who were the *sons of God?* This term *"sons of God"* in every other place where the expression is used in the Old Testament (Job 1:6, 2:1, 38:7; in Psalms 29:1, 89:6; and Daniel 3:25) the meaning is angels. So the angels found the females to be fair and took them for wives; that means they had sex with them, and they had offspring. It also infers that the offspring were giants and became man of great renown, such as the giant Goliath. But don't miss one item in this scripture, it says, *"And also after that."* What does that mean?

This event is called the "Second Influx." It happened after Noah's flood, after God drowned all the hybrids the first time. From the skeletal evidence found all over the world perhaps this "Influx" happened over and over again. What are we talking about here? We are talking about Fallen Angels. We're talking about supernatural beings in their supernatural bodies coming to earth from the dimension we call Heaven or Paradise, disobeying God's orders to be born of flesh. Instead, they took human women to be their wives and had children with them. These are the Fallen Angels of the Book of Jude. I hope you can see where this intersects with those misguided people who believe this is all about extraterrestrial beings from another planet. We are talking about supernatural beings from another dimension, and according to the Bible, they are coming back.

CHAPTER 9

Giants of the Bible

As we saw in the sixth chapter of Genesis, the sons of God, angels, were here on earth, and found the daughters of men to be very desirable. Genesis goes on to say that these angels took wives of whomever they wanted, of the daughters of man, and had children with them. Again, Genesis states very clearly in chapter 6 verse 4;

> *There were giants in the earth in those days; and also after that, when the sons of God came in unto the daughters of men, and they bear children to them, the same became mighty men which were of old, men of renown.*

Genesis goes on to state that it was because of this abomination in the eyes of God that He brought on the flood of Noah. But in this verse, it says, "And also after that," which tells us the Fallen Angels came back after the flood of Noah. It is also clear in biblical terms that the first influx was driven by Satan's desire to destroy the bloodline to Christ. It is clearly stated in Genesis that the reason Noah and his family were saved from the flood, was because they were the only descendants of Adam that had not interbred with the angels. As we're told in the sixth chapter of Genesis, verse 9:

> *These are the generations of Noah: Noah was a just man and perfect in his generations, and Noah walked with God.*

The word "perfect" in this verse is very important. It's word number 8435 in your Strong's, and it means *without blemish in their pedigree*, and it comes from the root word number 3205 in your Strong's which means *to bear young, show lineage, pedigree*. In other words, their lineage from Adam had not been tainted by these supernatural beings, and furthermore they were the only ones of which this was true. This unavoidably brings us to a Christian teaching of which I have no idea how it came to be. I know this is most controversial, but time is running out and God's truth needs to be trumpeted. I'll just say it straight out; Adam and Eve were not the first humans God put on this earth. The Bible doesn't even say that, in fact it says exactly the opposite. Yet from pulpits all over this world, the sheep are fed this lie that makes it very difficult to defend anything else in the Bible. Let me be very clear, when God is creating the heaven and the earth He does it in an exact progression. On the sixth day God creates male and female humankind, he blessed them and then told them:

> *Be fruitful, and multiply, and replenish the earth, and subdue it…*

And then according to Genesis 2:2, on the seventh day God rested. And then in Genesis 2:5, evidently on the next day, God looked around and saw He had not created a farmer:

> *There was not a man to till the ground.*

It seems pretty simple, if God realizes there is no farmer, the hunters and fishers must have already been created here on earth.

At that point, God *formed* Adam and Eve (Genesis 2:7). Do you understand what God is telling us? According to the Bible, God created men and women and told them to go multiply; they were the hunters and the fishers of the world. And then sometime after that, God started a new bloodline of farmers, who would also be the beginning of the bloodline to Messiah. Read Genesis with understanding and ask yourself some simple questions. If we have the account of every generation, documented in Genesis, from Adam to Noah, then Noah to David, and then David to Jesus Christ, where did all the other people in the world come from? These other people would not be possible if Adam was the first human created. We have the *Canaanites, and the Hittites, and the Hivites, and the Perizzites, and the Girgashites, and the Amorites, and the Jebusites* (Joshua 3:10), and all the other gentiles of the world, they are not mentioned in the bloodline of Adam. We have the different races, and we find people unrelated to Adam's bloodline living all over the world. Where did they all come from? It's clear, if you have eyes to see and ears to hear, they came from the sixth day creation, and God looked at them and saw *"It was very good."*

Somewhere in the world of theology and scholarship things have gone awry. Using common sense and the Scriptures, it is easy to see; Adam was the patriarch of the family that led to Isaac. Isaac had a son Jacob who had twelve sons, who were the patriarchs of the twelve tribes of Israel. We also have the Arab tribes accounted for through Ishmael the son of Abraham and Sarah's Egyptian maidservant, Hagar. That's it! Where do all these other people come from? Where do all the races come from? Obviously, they came from somewhere, and if you read your Bible carefully and with understanding, it will tell you they were created by God on the sixth day. Think about it, Genesis 4:16–17, even tells us that after killing Abel, Cain was banished from the Garden and went to the distant land of Nod where he took a wife. Where did these people come from? History has little to say about the early days of Cain and his descendants. Some attribute legendary figures such as Sargon the Magnificent to the bloodline of Cain, but the true descendants of Cain can be found in Genesis chapter 4 beginning in verse 17. Adam's genealogy, however, is then given in chapter 5 of Genesis and it is telling that Cain is not included in Adam's genealogy. This is because Cain was not Adam's son and was not part of the bloodline to Jesus Christ. Remember there are two fathers.

So giants roamed the earth in those days; they were still around even in the days of Moses. In Numbers chapter 13, the spies who were sent into the wilderness of Paran to Kadesh returned to Moses with talk of giants:

33 And there we saw giants, the sons of Anak, which come of the Giants: and we were in our own site as grasshoppers, and so we were in their sight.

Although these reports were later discredited, by Joshua and Caleb, telling Moses and the Israelites that the giants had already been destroyed, it is important to note, they in no way denied giants existed there before their arrival. If you are a Bible-believing Christian, then you have no choice; there were giants, and it's no surprise that we find skeletal remains of them today. This in no way means they are extraterrestrial in origin. In fact, it is interesting to note that these giants were the offspring of supernatural beings, but ultimately were of flesh in nature themselves. The offspring of the *daughters of men* and the *sons of God* were all ultimately flesh and blood, and for this reason, physical remains of them can be found here on earth today. On the other hand, the supernatural body is not of a flesh nature, and that is why physical remains of those creatures (angels) are not found.

The skeletal remains of giants across this globe are explained in the Bible, and it should be no surprise that we find them here on earth. Although the main plan of Satan was to destroy the blood-line to Christ that does not change the fact that Fallen Angels are attracted to human females. The Bible reports that they returned to earth and mated with human females after Noah's flood, perhaps several times, and their offspring tended to be very large.

As the tribes of Israel finally moved into the Promised Land, we still find evidence of the existence of giants. In the book of Deuteronomy chapter 3, we are told about the remnant of the giants:

11 For only Og King of Bashan remained of the remnant of giants; behold, his bedstead was a bedstead of iron; is it not in Rabbath of the children of Ammon? Nine cubits was the length thereof, and four cubits the breadth of it, after the cubit of a man.

The equivalent of a cubit in inches is up for debate, but for this example, let's use two feet per cubit. This giant's bed was then nine cubits or eighteen feet long and eight feet wide! Do giants walk the earth today? No, God took care of them. Whether by the flood of Noah, or through other means God made sure they would not survive. Perhaps they had problems reproducing, whatever the reason, while there are physical remains of these giants, they were not allowed to survive until today.

For a deeper study into the giants of the Old Testament, check out the word *Nephilim*, which means "*fallen ones*" and the scripture related to them. Check out the word translated *giants* in the fourth verse of Genesis chapter 6: "*Nephiyl*," it is the Hebrew word number 5303 in your Strong's. The meaning for the word is: *bully or tyrant; giant*. There is no hiding from the truth, the Bible explicitly states, and describes giants in many different places in the Old Testament. It is no surprise that these flesh descendants of the *sons of God* would leave physical remains behind. The fact that skeletal remains are discovered in various areas across the globe is evidence, I believe, the *sons of God* were not only attracted to the daughters of Adam, but to the daughters of all the races here on earth.

CHAPTER 10

Technology in the Bible

One of the things that excites ANCIENT ASTRONAUT THEORISTS most is the staggering amount of physical evidence all over the world that bolsters the claim that ancient cultures had technology far more sophisticated than ours today. The city of Atlantis is pictured as an ultramodern technology rich culture that dates back perhaps ten thousand years or more. One of their favorite theories is that the monoliths, including the Great Pyramid of Giza, formed a network or grid, by which power was transferred all over the world. What if it were true? Picture mounted on top of the Great Pyramid of Giza and on top of other pyramids all over the world, as well as many other monoliths worldwide, "power magnets" that could attract then transmit energy from monolith to monolith in patterns all over the globe. Picture big metal contraptions perhaps that could draw power out of natural sources worldwide and then transmit them to other parts of the globe. "The aliens" ANCIENT ASTRONAUT THEORISTS say, "took these devises with them when they left." Right or wrong, there are many other physical remains of ancient technology worldwide which is just as amazing and astounding as this idea.

We have no idea how the Egyptians cut the stones for the Great Pyramid of Giza, considering their size and the laser-perfect accuracy of the cuts, which is also true for many other sites worldwide. Today, even with our technology, we can't duplicate the thin cement used to glue the huge facing stones to the Pyramid's building blocks. No one can really explain how the giant stones were transported, the "current opinion" held by most mainstream experts is that the stones were rolled on logs. Yet there is no explanation of where the logs came from, or how they could have survived the weight of the gigantic stones. Experiments show the tremendous weight of the stones would have crushed the logs in the operation.

The extensive knowledge of the planets, stars, and solar systems that the ancients possessed is difficult to understand. How they arrived at this information and obtained the math knowledge needed for the calculations is a mystery. The ancients' ability to align monuments with other structures across the globe would need technology rivaling what we have today, yet there they sit perfectly aligned with each other. There are sites, including the Egyptian Pyramids, where residue has been found that indicates some type of high-tech explosion took place within the confines of their walls. The physical evidence really is overwhelming, I can't see how anyone with an open mind, looking at all the evidence, could conclude that this is all fantasy. There are hundreds and hundreds of examples where the only reasonable conclusion to how these monuments were constructed is modern technology.

It is important to remember that wondrous technology much more advanced than we've talked about here is discussed in the Bible. We discussed Noah's flood, can you imagine the technology, mathematics, and engineering knowledge it would take to build a ship that large? Yet this old boy Noah was able to pull it off. The instructions for its construction and its exact dimensions are laid out in the Bible. But it is difficult to get a real feel for the enormous size of the Ark from just reading the biblical account. An ambitious endeavor took place a few years ago in Grant County Williamstown, Kentucky. Now billed as the ARK ENCOUNTER, it is a full-sized "Noah's Ark," and is the largest timber frame structure in the world. The Ark was built in part by skilled Amish craftsmen, which leaves the question of how good old boy Noah was able to accomplish this feat. The Ark is 510 feet long and 85 feet wide, standing 51 feet high, and one visit to this incredible ship should bring into focus that technology must have been used in Noah's day.

Another example of amazing modern technology found in the Old Testament of the Bible is the Ark of the Covenant and it has been the topic of discussion and rumors for thousands of years. Recently you may remember, in the 1981 movie *Raiders of the Lost Ark*, Indiana Jones, along with the Germans, and a whole lot of other people were searching for the Ark. In the movie, you may remember, when the Germans removed the lid from the Ark some power emerged and melted the Germans' skin off their bones. This idea of the Ark containing some ominous power within it is based on biblical accounts. In the book of Joshua chapter's 3, 4, and 6, we are told of the amazing power of the Ark of the Covenant. In chapter 3 of Joshua, we are told,

> *3 And they commanded the People saying "When you see the ark of the covenant of the Lord your God, and the priests the Levites pairing it, then ye shall remove from your place, and go after it.*

> *4 Yet there shall be a space between you and it, about 2000 cubits by measure: come not near into it, that ye may know the way by which you must go: for you have not passed this way heretofore."*

> *5 And Joshua said unto the People, "Sanctify yourselves: for tomorrow the Lord will do wonders among you."*

Because of the ominous power unleashed from the Ark of the Covenant the Lord warns the people to stay back away from it, two thousand cubits using the previous average that would be about four thousand feet. What was going to happen out in front of the Israelites is comparable to what happened at the parting of the Red Sea. And Joshua encourages his people to cleanse themselves and repent from their sins. Joshua continues,

> *8 And thou shalt command the priests that bear the ark of the covenant, saying, "When ye are come to*

the brink of the water of Jordan, ye shall stand still in Jordan."

9 And Joshua said unto the children of Israel, "Come hither, and hear the words of the Lord your God."

10 And Joshua said, "Hereby you shall know that the living God is among you, and that He will without failed drive out from before you the Canaanites, and the Hittites, and the Hivites, and the Perizzites, and the Girgashites, and the Amorites, and the Jebusites.

After everything the Israelites had been through, from being led out of bondage in Egypt, to be taken care of for forty years while wandering around in the desert, you would think they would already know that the living God was among them. God is promising them that He is going before them and cleanse their new home of their enemies. The enormous power unleashed from the Ark of the Covenant would be devastating to their enemies. But first, the Lord is going to part the Jordan River for the Israelites.

11 Behold, the ark of the covenant, even the Lord of all the earth passes over before you into Jordan.

15 And as they that bear the ark were come unto Jordan, and the feet of the priests that bear the ark were dipped in the brim of the water (for Jordan overflow all his banks all the time of harvest,)

17 And the priests that bear the ark of the covenant of the Lord stood firm on dry ground in the midst of Jordan, and all the Israelites passed over on dry ground, until all the people were passed clean over Jordan.

In the sixth chapter of Joshua, the Lord instructs him exactly how the Israelites are to take the city of Jericho. Again, the Ark of the Covenant and the power that comes from within it is instrumental in conquering Jericho. Joshua was told to march once around the city for six days, and below their trumpets. But on the seventh day, the Israelites were instructed to march around the city seven times. In Joshua chapter 6 we are told,

> *15 And it came to pass on the seventh day, that they rose early about the dawning of the day, and compassed the city after the same manner seven times: only on that day they compassed the city seven times.*

> *16 And it came to pass at the seventh time, when the priests blew with the trumpets, Joshua said unto the people, Shout; for the Lord hath given you the city.*

> *20 So the people shouted when the priests blew with the trumpets: and it came to pass, when the people heard the sound of the trumpet, and the people shouted with a great shout, that the wall fell down flat, so that the people went up into the city, every man straight before him, and they took the city.*

Once again, the power of the Ark of the Covenant is on display. Marching around the walls of Jericho carrying the Ark of the Covenant, blowing their trumpets, seven times, and then the power of the Ark was unleashed. The walls of Jericho fell to the ground; tell me that's not some powerful technology. Remember God Himself, instructed Moses exactly how to construct the Ark. It is important to remember that God instructed the Israelites to go into the Promised Land leading with the Ark of the Covenant and promised them that the power of His glory would go before them and destroy their enemies. We should note that many things about the instructions given to Moses lead experts to believe that some type of electrical charge was carried by the Ark. The handlers of the Ark were given exact instructions on what and what not to do when they were transporting the Ark of the Covenant. Transporters of the Ark were warned to be diligent about wearing the necessary garments during transportation.

A few years after the parting of the River Jordan, the Ark had been at Shiloh and the elders of Israel decided to take the Ark onto the battlefield to assist them in a battle against the Philistines. As usual Israel failed to put God in the equation, and never asked Him for His blessing in the battle or even asked Him whether they should go into battle. They were dramatically defeated and lost thirty thousand men. The Ark was captured by the Philistines and was taken to several Philistine cities before it ended up in Ashdod. In chapters 5 and 6 of 1 Samuel the story is told of how the giant statue of Dagon, god of the Philistines, was subjugated to the Ark of the Covenant. The Philistines were also physically plagued by the Ark with tumors and boils and hemorrhoids and infestations, until they returned the Ark seven months later to the Israelites. This technological marvel, known as the Ark of the Covenant, could through God inflict pain, misery, disease, and ultimately death upon the enemies of Israel. It had the power to part the River Jordan, and defeat Israel's enemies on the battlefield. But wait, there was even more to the marvelous technology of the Ark of the Covenant.

It may not seem as glorious as the Ark's ability to bring death and destruction upon Israel's enemies, but through the Ark Moses and the children of God were able to commune directly with God Himself. In the twenty-fifth chapter of Exodus, Moses is given the exact dimensions to which the Ark is to be built, the material that it is to be built from, and the way it is to be finished with gold. Moses is told to cast four rings of gold to be put at each corner, and the rings of gold were to support staves overlaid with gold that would be used to carry the Ark. Moses is also told to put the Testimony (the Ten Commandments) inside the Ark of the Covenant. Then Moses is told to put a Mercy seat of pure gold on top and was given what its exact dimensions were to be. Moses was also told by God to make two cherubim of gold, to be placed at each end of the Mercy seat. In Exodus chapter 25 God gives His instructions to Moses:

> *20 And the cherubim shall stretch forth their wings on high, covering the Mercy seat with their wings, and their faces shall look one to another; toward the mercy seat shall the faces of the cherubim be.*

> *21 And thou shalt put the mercy seat above upon the ark; and in the ark thou shalt put the Testimony that I shall give thee.*

> *22 And there I will meet with thee, and I will commune with thee from above the mercy seat, from between the two cherubim's which are upon the Ark of the Testimony, of all things which I will give thee in commandment unto the children of Israel.*

Think about this statement for a minute, God not only promises that he is going to commune with the children of Israel on earth, but he tells Moses how to use the Ark to communicate directly with Him. And Moses does communicate with God.

> *89 And when Moses was gone into the tabernacle of the congregation to speak with Him, then he heard the voice of one speaking unto him from off the mercy seat that was upon the ark of Testimony, from between the two cherubims: and He spake unto him.* (Numbers 7:89)

There is no denying that sounds like advanced communication technology, but in the first chapter of the Book of Ezekiel, we are introduced to another technology even more amazing, and perhaps more relevant to those of us living on earth today. When examining Ezekiel's account in chapter 1, we must remember that the man telling the story had seen no form of transportation more advanced than a cart pulled by a donkey. Taking that into consideration, Ezekiel's account of God's vehicle, which also transported his physical throne, is excellent.

First, we should consider the subject of wings and how they are used in Scripture. Have you ever noticed that most pictures, paintings, and illustrations of angels down through the centuries depict these supernatural beings as having wings? Usually in Scripture an angel appears to be a young male around twenty or thirty. No wings. Consider the destruction of Sodom and Gomorrah, the angels that came to destroy that city didn't have wings. The angel of the Lord, when wrestling Jacob, didn't have wings, in fact most depictions of angels in Scripture do not include wings. The angels waiting for Mary Magdalene and the other women at Jesus's tomb were not described as having wings. Although many of the paintings depicting this event show the angels with wings, the verse in the Bible describing the event says nothing about wings. In fact, in Hebrews chapter 13 it states:

2 Be not forgetful to entertain strangers; for thereby some have entertained angels unawares.

The word *"entertain"* in the Greek means to be hospitable, in other words you better be nice to strangers because you never know when there may be an angel around, in fact the stranger maybe an angel. That doesn't sound much like a winged creature, I think I would notice wings.

There are exceptions, however; one would be the depiction of the two gold cherubim a top the Ark of the Covenant we just discussed. The depiction of these two cherubim demonstrated their role, they protect the Mercy seat or throne of God. Do some or all cherubim have wings? I don't know…maybe, but we do know cherubim are not ordinary angels. Most of the time, however, I believe these depictions of supernatural beings with wings comes from the ancient idea that for an angel to come from heaven it must fly here. At that time, in order to fly, you had to have wings, therefore the artists that created the paintings and illustrations of angels added wings to them to demonstrate their ability to fly. We also see this throughout the Old Testament when the "Vehicles of God" are described.

In Ezekiel's account of God's vehicle in chapter 1, he describes it as having wings. His description is different from the descriptions of the angels, however, he described this object as having four wings that were folded up into each other (Ezekiel 1:23). This makes me think of my pet cockatiel, and how he folds his wings up into his body. If a circular object was to have four wings equally distributed around its circumference, they could fold up together forming a tight circle, like a saucer. If you were Ezekiel and had experienced only what Ezekiel had experienced, it would seem logical that anything that flew must have wings.

Ezekiel's account is amazing, he describes the ship as a wheel inside a wheel (Ezekiel 1:16), with landing gears (Ezekiel 1:24), with portholes or windows in the craft (Ezekiel 1:18), and even states that he sees living creatures inside the vehicle (Ezekiel 1:19–21). Ezekiel also does an amazing job of describing the movement of the vehicle, especially having never seen anything like this before. He talks about how the vehicle moves whatever way it wants, which is unlike what he's used to; a donkey pulling a cart. Where the donkey's head went the cart would follow, but in this vehicle, it went right, left, up or down. The wheel inside a wheel went anyway it wanted, and the living creatures inside went with it. And then, from inside that vehicle was brought the physical throne of God.

CHAPTER 11

Flying Saucers in the Bible

When the subject of UFOs came up, a teacher of mine would always say that it depended on who was driving them, as to whether they were good or bad. He of course was not talking about crafts piloted by extraterrestrial beings from another planet. He was talking about supernatural beings, angels; good ones and bad ones, traveling in vehicles from the dimension we call Heaven or Paradise to this dimension of flesh in which we live. Perhaps the most amazing example of advanced technology I can point to in the Old Testament is the Wheels inside of Wheels in Ezekiel, and the Fiery Chariots of God and God's Whirlwind in 2 Kings 2:1–12, among other places.

> *And it came to pass, as they still went on, and talked,*
> *that behold, there appeared a chariot of fire, and horses*
> *of fire, and parted them both asunder; and Elijah went*
> *up by a whirlwind into heaven.* (2 Kings 2:11)

Make no mistake, Elijah wasn't taken away by a big gust of wind, he was taken away in a vehicle described as a *chariot of fire*. And then in the book of Isaiah chapter 66, prophesying about the End Times, Isaiah says,

> *15 For behold, the Lord will come with fire, and*
> *with his chariots like a whirlwind, to render his*
> *anger with fury, And his rebuke with flames of fire.*

With his chariots like a whirlwind, not a physical whirlwind, but *like a whirlwind.* But perhaps the most startling Scripture that really brings everything into focus when speaking of this technology in the Old Testament is found in the Book of 2 Kings chapter 6. The king of Syria is at war with Israel, and we find Elisha has been advising the king of Israel about the king of Syria's plans. The king of Syria sent an army of men with horses and chariots to capture Elisha (2 Kings 6:14.) Then,

> *15 And when the servant of the man of God was risen early, and gone forth, behold, a host compassed the city both with horses and chariots. And his servant said unto him, alas, my master, how shall we do?*

Elisha's servant was worried, and rightfully so, the two men were no match for this large army. Elisha's servant is asking him what they will do to avoid total annihilation.

> *16 And he answered, fear not: for they that be with us are more than they that be with them.*

In other words, Elisha was telling his servant; "Don't worry, our boys can take their boys." But in Elisha's servant's mind it was only the two of them!

> *17 And Elisha prayed, and said Lord, I pray thee, open his eyes that he may see. The Lord opened the eyes of the young man; and he saw: and behold, the mountain was full of horses and chariots of fire roundabout Elisha.*

A multitude was there to do battle with the Elisha's enemies, Chariots of Fire, ready to rain destruction down upon Elisha's enemies. The sky was filled with Wheels inside of Wheels, and like a whirlwind God spread among the enemies of Elisha and struck them blind. Imagine the technology on display to Elisha's young servant. Imagine the firepower there that was available to fight Elisha's enemies.

Another example of advanced technology in the Bible, is the Star of Bethlehem that led the Holy Men form the east to the place where the Christ child was staying. Think about the story, the wise men from the east had been traveling, following the "star" for months, day and night. In Matthew chapter 2, after the wisemen had spoken to King Herod it states,

> *9 When they had heard the king, they departed; and lo, the star, which they saw in the east, went before them, till it came and stood over where the young child was.*

Until the twentieth century, the observance of a light in the sky automatically led one to conclude it was a star or planet. The idea of a flying vehicle with a bright light on it was unimaginable to people because they had no experience to support that idea. For the Wise Men to describe the light they were following as a star was only natural, also it had been prophesied in the ancient scriptures. What if the star was one of God's fiery chariots, or one of His Wheels inside a Wheel instead of a star? When was the last time you saw a star that was visible all night and all day, and moved in one direction slow enough for you to follow it? I'm not sure how the ANCIENT ASTRONAUT THEORISTS would react to this verse. Would they say that somehow extraterrestrials were involved with the birth of Jesus Christ? Probably.

Erich von Daniken in his book *Gods from Outer Space* proposed some forward-thinking ideas about space craft and their evolution. Propulsion is of course the basic problem in space exploration and von Daniken in 1970 made an interesting observation about the design of spacecraft and the type of propulsion they would need to be successful. The type of space travel that von Daniken envisioned in his book has not yet materialized, some would argue that the United States by backing away from space exploration after our successful moon landings, caused a lack of advancement in the field of space travel. Once again, I have to ask the question; have you ever wondered why we haven't gone back to the moon? The type of propulsion that we have now, as von Daniken rightfully points out, has major limitations and problems, and is not adequate for the type of space travel most envision for the future. In his book *Gods from Outer Space*, in chapter 5, von Daniken states,

> The liberation of higher propulsive energy is the key that would lead to the manufacture of new types of spacecraft. The time when technology will have as yet incredible energies at its disposal is no longer so far away. When that time comes, it could lead to pure photon propulsion units that reach a velocity close to the speed of light and can provide propulsion for almost an unlimited period.
>
> Then we should no longer have to economize on every pound of payload, as we do today, when for every pound that a spacecraft takes on a journey to the moon, an extra 2590 pounds of fuel is needed. Once that were the case, spacecraft would soon be built in a very different shape.
>
> Old text and archaeological finds around the world have convinced me that the first spacecraft that reached the earth many thousands of years ago were spherical, and I am sure that the spacecraft of the future will, once again, will be spherical.

Obviously, things have not moved as fast as von Daniken envisioned, but I must admit that if the thrust of the United States space program had continued on the path of manned flights, spacecraft would have likely evolved much more than they have so far. Instead, the space program focused on small vehicles sent on unmanned flights to explore distant planets within our solar system. Seems logical to find out as much as we can with unmanned flights, especially considering factors like the cost and the danger to life. But what about those strange-looking objects, and lights, and other bizarre and weird things people see up in the sky?

In March 2018, a United States Navy report about a UFO sighting was declassified; in 2015, two Navy pilots made a sighting of some type of "alien" craft near the United States East Coast. The pilots were flying Boeing F/A-18 super hornet fighter jets, when they sighted what they described as; an oval shaped object hovering above the sea. The F/A-18s were traveling at twenty-five thousand feet, and when they flew lower to have a look at the object, one of the pilots, David Fravor said, "it accelerated like nothing I've seen before." Fravor said, "It had no (exhaust) plumes, wings or rotors and out ran our F-18s." The "alien" craft was also picked up by independent radar and pictures have been released from the Department of Defense that clearly show the object on the radar screen. Also, ABC news.com released a thirty-five-second video recording, which they say was captured by an infrared camera aboard one of the F-18 fighter jets. Reports say the "alien" craft followed the jet fighters almost all the way to the West Coast before accelerating at an immeasurable speed away from the planes.

On March 22, 2018, in an area near Jacksonville, Florida, a large silver craft was sighted as it moved straight up in the air and then disappeared. The triangle object was silver in color and appeared to have circular objects at each of the two corners facing west. On the corner pointing east, there appeared to be a black area going across the end shaped like a ruler. On March 25, 2018, around Ixtapa, Zihuantanejo, Mexico an entire family, and other people, saw a bright red light, which momentarily would turn white and then quickly red again in the night sky. The light was very clear and moved vertically and then suddenly horizontally at a very high speed and continued to make unusual movements in the sky. The light was red most of the time with an intermittent short white burst of light. On March 26, 2018, in the area around Halifax, Nova Scotia, Canada, a triangle formation of white lights that would grow bright and then dim and then grow bright again was observed by a local husband and wife. The couple estimated the height of the triangle to be around one hundred thousand feet from the ground, this is over three times the height that most aircraft fly. On March 27, 2018, around Puyallup, Washington, a red object traveling west to east just below the clouds was reported. It was first noticed in the late afternoon, around dinnertime, and was traveling faster than a plane, but was visible for several seconds. These are just a few of the sightings reported between the March 22, 2018, and the end of March 2018.

I think it's safe to say; UFO sightings are not going away anytime soon. And now, when we see lights in the sky, we no longer automatically think it is a star or some planet. I believe Erich von Daniken is on to something, we just disagree on who is piloting these UFOs. Von Daniken questions why God would need a vehicle to travel, I ask why wouldn't He? The Bible leaves no doubt that angels travel between the dimension of heaven and the dimension where we live. The Bible tells us that archangels have come to earth, cherubim have come to earth, and other angels that were simply messengers from God, have come down to earth. Satan himself, traveled back and forth from one dimension to the other. It states so in Job chapter 1:

> *6 Now there was a day when the sons of God came to present themselves before the Lord, and Satan came also among them.*
>
> *7 And the Lord said unto Satan, Whence comest thou? Then Satan answered the Lord and said from going to and fro in the earth, and from walking up and down in it.*

Let me ask you a question: How did Satan get to earth? Did he have wings and fly? Or do you think he might have come in a vehicle made to travel between dimensions? My money is on the vehicle. The same is also true for all the other angels in the Bible; did they fly down here to earth using their wings? Or do you think they might have traveled here in a very high-tech vehicle?

PART THREE

THE GREAT
DECEPTION

CHAPTER 12

The New Lie

Darwin's Theory of Evolution has been proven false by several new discoveries concerning DNA, but we don't see this news broadcast to the world. The process of Natural Selection is not an evolutionary process, and the Theory of Evolution will never become a Law of Science. The Theory of Evolution is riddled with falsehoods, and while the DNA in different plants or animals allows, the use of selective breeding to produce a new "breed" or "type," it never happens between species. Selective breeding is used in dogs and fish for example to create new breeds and it is used to produce new types of flowers, fruits and vegetables. Evolutionists, however, refuse to admit that there is no proof any species of any type, plant or animal, has ever evolved into a different species. They are still looking.

Natural selection is obviously a lie; the evidence leads us in the opposite direction. Evolutionists point to melanin in the skin and claim it is a natural sunscreen that evolved in greater amounts in the skin of darker-skinned people living near the Equator. The same evolutionists ignore the darker-skinned Eskimos who live north of the Arctic Circle. The people of the old Soviet Union and from Nordic countries have light skin, light hair, and blue eye color. If natural selection was true, Eskimos and people of other northern areas would have thicker skin and maybe fur covering their bodies. Humans living in the tropics predominately have very dark skin rather than some type of reflective skin that would keep them cooler and protect them from the damaging effects of sunlight at the same time. Instead, black skin absorbs heat more than white skin, reality is the opposite of what they claim; the whole thing is a lie.

Things with great complexity do not happen by chance, anywhere in nature. There is an old fable that claims if you set a monkey at a typewriter for long enough, it will eventually randomly type out the Gettysburg Address; this just is not true. Yet this very claim is used to defend the idea that our universe started by chance. If their claim was true, it would mean that all the structured and complex things in the universe, which all adhere to the Laws of Nature and Mathematics, happened by chance. It is ridiculous, in fact studies have shown that the more things change the simpler they become, because complexity is "evolved" out of them. Higher education pushes the lies of evolution and natural selection, and the world scientific community swears to them.

There is other physical evidence we see all over the world that disproves the Theory of Evolution. Petrified remains of cockroaches millions of years old are the same as their modern-day ancestors, not evolved at all. There are many other examples, the coelacanth fish is one. The coelacanth fish was called a prime transitional example of evolution for decades, equipped with primitive lungs and half-developed legs poised to move out of the water onto land. This fake scientific narrative in support of evolution was destroyed when a coelacanth fish was netted off the coast of South Africa, the fish was exactly like the 350-million-year-old fossil. Seems they had been common in those waters for years; overnight the coelacanth fish goes from being false evidence of evolution to being absolute proof that evolution is a lie; 350 million years of no change in the coelacanth fish does not speak well for the Theory of Evolution.

If evolution were true and was an ongoing continual process occurring over millions of years as we have been told, we would have discovered millions of transitional fossils by now. We should be able to go out into the world we live in and see living animals that are in the state of transition from one species to another, they would have partially developed features and partially developed organs. There is no evidence, it does not exist; the complete absence of transitional fossils in the fossil record and the lack of living transitional animals in the real world should have put an end to the Theory of Evolution years ago. Instead, what we see in the fossil record is a sudden explosion of fully formed complex life. This sudden appearance of complex life in the fossil record, without any evolutionary history, is undeniable. Still, children continue to be taught in schools all over the world that evolution is a scientific fact; and so, the lie continues.

A little-known fact is that Darwin's Theory of Evolution has pagan roots that go back thousands of years. The ancient Greeks, Hindus, Egyptians, and Babylonians believed in different types of evolution. Just as evolution has become a religion to the evolutionists of today, in ancient times their evolutionary beliefs became their religion. From the Greek philosopher Epicurus's belief that the universe came about through the chance movement of small invisible particles to the Hindu belief that creation occurred like a seed springing forth, evolution of some sort is at the root of their beliefs. Showing the way for the evolutionists of today, the ancient evolutionists also refused to address the ultimate question; if their beliefs were true where did the small invisible particles or the original seed like material come from in the first place?

This "elephant in the room" is also the most glaring example of the complicity between higher education and science perpetuating the lie. They hide the truth about evolution from the world, by their continuing refusal to address the question of the origin of matter. Where did matter come from? How did it come to exist in the first place? If the "Big Bang" really happened, where did the matter come from for it to "Bang"? Evolutionists have no answer to the question of matter because there is none, so they continue to just tell a lie and ignore the obvious.

Question: Why doesn't the world scientific community just tell us the truth?

Answer: If we didn't evolve from the monkeys, then science and the evolutionists must come up with another answer to the question of where we came from and how we got here. People are still highly invested in the Theory of Evolution, but that can't last for long, not with the growing amount of contradictory scientific information that is emerging. Just as the scientists of old had to admit the world was not flat, someday the lie of evolution will eventually be put to rest. Before that happens, a new explanation must be created, or evolutionists and the scientific community will have to admit Creation by God is the only reasonable answer. Imagine a world with no other explanation of our existence! The entirety of their world view would disappear, but they won't let that happen, not if they can help it.

So the twenty-first century lie is that humans are the product of experimentation by super-intelligent advanced extraterrestrials from another planet, in another solar system…in another galaxy far, far, away. Just as we are told in the movie *Star Wars*, the scientific community assures us that the universe must be teaming with intelligent life, even though we haven't made contact with any. At the same time, seculars tell us it is idiotic and self-indulgent to think we might be the only intelligent life in the entire universe. I'm sorry but the math doesn't support their theory. In fact, it supports the opposite, as we learn more about life; the larger the list gets of things that are absolutely necessary for life to exist. Currently, the list of things needed for life to exist on a planet tops 150 separate items or conditions, all of which are needed at the same time. The truth is the odds are against the existence of life, even on this planet. But science continues telling their lie; the universe must be teaming with life and it is inevitable we will make contact with alien intelligent life someday. Extraterrestrials are out there, they tell us, they must be…and they may have been here on earth before…and they may even be our ancestors! The new theology of extraterrestrials developing human life on earth through experimentation is being developed, polished, and advanced every day through our educational systems and the world media.

It is important to understand why this is happening now, and why understanding this lie is so critical for Christians everywhere. It is necessary for Christians to stand against the lie of evolution but also this new lie against Creation. It is important to make this stand now more than ever before, because if this is the last generation spoken of by Christ, then this new lie is most likely part of the final deception of Revelation 20:3.

In the thirteenth chapter of Mark, the Parable of the Fig Tree is introduced in the New Testament by Jesus Christ. Jesus doesn't just recommend that we know and understand the Parable of the Fig Tree, He was a little more forceful.

28 Now learn a parable of the fig tree; when her branch is yet tender, and putteth forth leaves, ye know that summer is near:

29 So ye in like manner when ye shall see these things come to pass, know that it is nigh, even at the door.

"Now learn" is an order, and yet from my experience I expect many of you reading those two verses have no idea what the Parable of the Fig Tree is or what it means. Don't feel bad, you are not alone, and it is not too late to learn! Jesus Christ Himself told us to learn it, maybe Christians should take this command seriously. It's so important that I feel it is my duty, for fear you don't do the work yourself, to show you what the basics of this parable are. Even if you are not familiar with the parable itself, you may have heard a preacher/teacher in some Christian setting, talk about how important the reestablishment of Israel was on May 14, 1948. But have you heard that the re-establishment of Israel may have signaled the beginning of the last generation? This statement is based upon the Parable of the Fig Tree, so let's take a close look at the parable Christ told us to learn.

The Parable begins in the Book of Jeremiah chapter 24, where the Lord showed Jeremiah two baskets of figs, one basket of good figs, and a second basket of very bad or evil figs. Remember, there are two fathers. And then the Lord likens the good figs to those of Judah who were carried away into captivity by Nebuchadnezzar. I hope you are developing a feeling for who those people were that are represented by the basket of very bad, evil figs. They look just like the good figs, and they were carried away into captivity too. Then in verse 6 of chapter 24, the Lord tells Jeremiah that after scattering Judah across the face of the earth, He will someday bring them back again to the Promised Land. The bad figs would naturally come back with them, but how would you know who was who? The answer is found in the difference between the wheat and the tares, and the fruit they bare when they mature. I don't think many serious Bible scholars would deny that this prophecy was most likely fulfilled in 1948, when the modern state of Israel was established.

In the thirteenth chapter of Mark, Jesus said that when we see the Parable of the Fig Tree fulfilled everything, He had just talked about would come to pass before that generation ended. There's some disagreement on how long a generation is, but there are only three generations discussed in the Bible, and in each instance a generation refers to how long people lived at that time. Therefore, it only makes sense that a modern generation would be the normal lifespan of the people living at this time. There is also some question about the fulfillment of the Parable of the Fig Tree happening in 1948, a few say that Israel really didn't control the Temple Mount in Jerusalem until the end of the Six-Day War on June 11, 1967. Whichever date you choose, or if you choose any date in between, you must conclude that the last generation already has quite a few gray hairs on it. But what exactly is going to be fulfilled in this generation of the Parable of the Fig Tree? What will be fulfilled is everything that Jesus prophesied in Mark 13 just before he told us to learn the Parable of the Fig Tree. Let's look at what Jesus said was going to be happening at the time of His return in the Book of Mark chapter 13:

5 (Jesus) Answering them began to say, take heed least any man deceives you:

6 For many shall come in my name saying, I am Christ; and shall deceive many.

Jesus is worried about us being deceived. What is the most important bit of information, Christ gave us that will keep us from being deceived? In my opinion, hands down, it is the fact that Satan comes first as the false Christ. We're told this in many places in the Bible from the Book of Daniel to the Book of Revelation. Satan will be released on to earth for a short period, five months according to the Book of Mark, and he is determined to prove himself to be God. This will be the most dangerous time in the history of Christianity, if you worship Satan as the returned Messiah you will be in jeopardy of eternal death. If you don't know the wicked one is coming first, you are going to be easy pickings for Satan. Christ doesn't want us to under estimate the power of this false Messiah or his power of deception. In the Book of Daniel, it is stated that the time of deception would be three and one-half years leading up to Satan's appearance and then after the appearance of Antichrist there would be another three and one-half years before the true Christ returns.

God was so concerned about His children and the intensity of this terrible deception; the time Satan is allowed to tempt God's children was shortened. In the Book of Matthew chapter 24, Christ tells us,

> *21 For then shall be great tribulation, such as was not since the beginning of the world to this time, no, nor ever shall be.*

> *22 And except those days should be shortened, there should no flesh be saved: but for the elect's sake those days shall be shortened.*

The deception is going to be so convincing, so powerful, the pressure from others will be so great, it will be very difficult to stand against Satan's lies unless you know the truth. If you know Satan comes first as the false Messiah, and if you know that he will be beautiful just as he is described in the Bible, and that he will be claiming to be Christ, you will not be tempted. To the contrary, you'll find him and his Fallen Angels disgusting, because you will know who they are and what they are doing. You need to know what will be going on just before this high-intensity deception begins, let's go back to Matthew 24:

> *6 And when ye shall hear of wars and rumors of wars, be not troubled: for such things must needs be; but the end shall not yet be.*

7 For nation shall rise against nation, and kingdom against kingdom: and there shall be famines, and pestilence, and earthquakes in divers places.

8 All these are the beginnings of sorrows.

Does this sound familiar to you? It should, this has been the situation ever sense Judah was returned to her homeland in 1948. Christ couldn't be clearer about what will be going on before he returns, it describes what has been going on for more than seventy years. But then in Matthew 24, Christ tells us what our purpose is in all of this:

9 Then shall they deliver you up to be afflicted and shall kill you: and ye shall be hated of all nations for my name's sake.

10 And then shall many be offended, and shall betray one another, and shall hate one another.

11 And many false prophets shall rise and shall deceive many.

12 And because iniquity shall abound, the love of many shall wax cold.

13 But he that shall endure unto the end, the same shall be saved.

These are very scary words to most people, but to the elect it speaks to their souls and assures them it is their destiny. These verses frighten many people because of the threat of affliction, and it says they will be killed. A good student of God's word will remember in the Book of Luke chapter 21 God gives us reason to be fearless. As he is telling his disciples all things that will be happening at this time, Christ says in Luke 11:

18 But there shall not a hair of your head parish.

19 In your patience possess ye your souls.

CHAPTER 13

The Desolator

Are you an End Times disciple of Christ? These two verses from the eleventh chapter of Luke are very important; take them to heart. Number 1, God promises you Satan shall not harm one hair on your head when you are testifying at this time. And number 2, always remember to be patient and trust in God's word. Remember the Parable of the Ten Virgins; it was the midnight hour when the five virgins ran out of oil causing them to miss the wedding. We need to stay strong until the midnight hour arrives; by the way, midnight at the time of Christ was not the end of the day. The Bible states that Satan is coming back as the Antichrist before the true Christ returns; the word *Antichrist* correctly translated means "instead of Christ." Satan will not be killing people that don't believe in him, although being a Christian these days can be dangerous, especially in some foreign countries. Think about it, how many Christians would Satan be able to convert if he goes around killing Christians? The killing is going to be done to the souls of God's children who are not prepared and accept Satan as Christ. Satan is not going to be killing physical bodies, but he will kill many souls with his deception and lies.

It is at this time, at this moment that God's elect will stand and embrace their destiny. The Holy Spirit will be here in full force ahead of the return of Christ and will take control of the situation. Also, the Two Witnesses will have been here on earth a short time before Satan is kicked out of heaven; down to earth. Most of the world will be worshiping Antichrist, but God's elect, not being deceived, will allow the Holy Spirit to speak God's truth through them. You are warned not to contemplate what you will say; you have nothing to do with it after you turn yourself over. We are to turn our entire being over to the Holy Spirit at this time. In the Book of Mark chapter 13, Jesus states,

> *11 But when they shall lead you, and deliver you up, take no thought beforehand what ye shall speak, neither do ye premeditate: but whatsoever shall be given you in that hour, that speak ye: for it is not ye that speak, but the Holy Ghost.*

This is the time of the Unforgivable Sin that many Christians worry themselves sick over. It is impossible to have committed it yet, and only the elect will be in jeopardy. The "Unforgivable Sin" is to be a member of the elect and deny the Holy Spirit access to speak through you, against Satan, during this time of the trials. I don't believe this will happen, the elect will know the false Christ from the true Christ, and they will do everything they can to defeat Satan. But there will be many others that participate in the Great Apostasy, or as the King James calls it the *falling away*. There will be many who believe the flood of lies of the false Messiah, as Paul states in 2 Thessalonians chapter 2:

> *3 Let no man deceive you by any means: for that day shall not come, except there come a falling away first, and that man of sin be revealed, the son of perdition,*
>
> *4 Who opposeth and exalteth himself above all that is called God, or that is worshiped; so that he as God sitteth in the temple of God, shewing himself that he is God.*

These verses give us great insight into the entity that will initiate and bring to fulfillment the Great Falling Away or Apostasy. Do you remember what *perdition* means and who the *son of perdition* is? In the Greek section of your Strong's concordance the word *perdition* is number 684 and means *spiritual eternal damnable, destruction, die, to perish, waste.* There is only one entity in the entirety of the Bible who has already been condemned, by name to spiritual/eternal death that would be Satan. So don't let some false teacher deceive you, telling you some human being is going to be posing as Christ, it is going to be Satan himself, in his beautiful supernatural body with all his supernatural power, perhaps claiming to be Christ returned. He will be in the holiest city on earth, Jerusalem, sitting on the throne of God on the Temple Mount, claiming to be God. Christ spoke of this event himself in Matthew 24, speaking of the time just before He returns, when He said;

> *15 When you therefore shall see the abomination of desolation, spoken of by Daniel the prophet, stand in the holy place (whoso readeth, let him understand)*

This term *abomination of desolation* would be better translated, as it was in the Moffatt Bible, as the "abominable desolator." What exactly does Daniel say about this desolator? Let's look to the eighth chapter in the Book of Daniel for the answer.

> *13 Then I heard one saint speaking, and another saint said unto that certain saint which spake, how long shall be the vision concerning the daily sacrifice, and the transgression of desolation, to give both the sanctuary and the host to be trodden underfoot?*

The daily sacrifice is communion, it will be ended and trodden underfoot because the world will be worshiping and taking communion to the false Christ. The transgression of desolation as previously stated is the transgression of the desolator, Satan, when he presents himself as God in the Temple of God in Jerusalem. Then, in this eighth chapter of Daniel, we are given a description of the Desolator and the fallen angels he brings with him:

23 And in the latter time of their kingdom, when the transgressors are come to the full, a king of fierce countenance, and understanding dark sentences, shall stand up.

24 And his power shall be mighty, but not by his own power: and he shall destroy wonderfully, and shall prosper, and practice, and shall destroy the mighty and the holy people.

25 And through his policy also he shall cause craft to prosper in his hand; and he shall magnify himself in his heart, and by peace shall destroy many: he shall also stand up against the Prince of princes; but he shall be broken without hand.

When his time is running short, remember he will only have five months, Satan as Antichrist will be cast to earth and present himself to the entire world as the returned Messiah. Again, Antichrist doesn't mean against Christ, it means instead of Christ. Don't underestimate his power, you are being warned, he will prosper, and he will fiercely attack God's children spiritually. This word *craft* is an important word, it is Strong's number 4820 in the Hebrew and comes from number 7411, and means Satan will be making *loud deceiving proclamations, committing fraud.* He will be lying to the people, but he will also be lying to himself, convincing himself he is as powerful as God. Don't ever forget the end of verse 25, Daniel says he will use peace to destroy God's children. He's going to come in peacefully and prosperously, playing the role of Messiah. He's not going to be killing people, in the beginning he's going to be understanding and forgiving, offering to help you in the fleshly challenges of this world. He may pay your bills, bring new technology to our daily life, and offer everlasting life, all you need to do is worship him as God. He will be beautiful, convincing, and powerful in ways we've never seen. Many will believe him and try to convince their friends and relatives, loved ones and neighbors, to worship this

Messiah. It will be the most dangerous times spiritually, in the history of mankind. Matthew 24 says,

> *10 And then shall many be offended, and shall betray one another, and shall hate one another.*

> *11 And many false prophets shall rise and shall deceive many.*

> *12 And because iniquity shall abound, the love of many shall wax cold.*

> *13 But he that shall endure until the end, the same shall be saved.*

It will be a very dangerous time, while not so much physically, it will be very dangerous spiritually. Satan is after your soul, and he is determined to win it by getting you to worship him. Don't do it! Don't let the false prophets or his preachers deceive you, endure until the end, until the midnight hour, and you shall be saved. In 1 Timothy chapter 4 God speaks of this time through Paul:

> *1 Now the Spirit speaketh expressly, that in the latter times some shall depart from the faith, giving heed to seducing spirits, and doctrines of devils;*

> *2 Speaking lies in hypocrisy, having their conscience seared with a hot iron;*

> *3 Forbidding to marry, and commanding to abstain from meats, which God hath created to be received with thanksgiving of them which believe and know the truth.*

CHAPTER 14

The Great Falling Away

They will be convincing, seducing you with Satan's new doctrine, his new religion. It will be the greatest revival this earth has ever seen. Why would marriage be forbidden? We may have already seen the answer in the Book of Genesis; the fallen angels have always been very attracted to women, they will want as many as possible for themselves. Satan and his angels will provide their followers with all their fleshly needs, all they will have to do is worship the False Savior. I can't overstate how dangerous of a time spiritually this will be, Hebrews chapter 6 states,

> *4 It is impossible for those who were once enlightened, and have tasted the heavenly gift, and were made partakers of the Holy Ghost,*
>
> *5 And have tasted the good word of God, and the powers of the world to come,*
>
> *6 If they shall fall away, to renew them again unto repentance; seeing they crucified to themselves the son of God afresh and put him to an open shame.*

This is the only place in the Bible where God withdraws forgiveness from one of His children other than when He condemned Satan to everlasting death. This is the Unforgivable Sin;

for a member of the elect, to refuse the Holy Spirit access to speak through them against the false Messiah, thereby turning against God, worshiping Satan, and essentially crucifying Christ again. As I've said, I don't believe this will happen, once a member of the elect truly understands who the false Messiah is, he or she will find him abominable. But beware and pray for those biblically illiterate Christians that will be duped, the deception is upon us and is growing. And God makes it very clear in the first chapter of Galatians that it is our duty to spurn and avoid false teaching and false teachers. If someone is teaching any doctrine that does not agree with Holy Scripture, it is false doctrine and the teacher is a false teacher. Paul took it personal when his disciples followed false teachers and false doctrine, in Galatians chapter 1 Paul states,

> *6 I marvel that you are so soon removed from him that called you into the grace of Christ unto another gospel:*

Paul is speaking about himself here and his disciples who followed other teachers, teaching false doctrine.

> *7 Which is not another; but there be some that trouble you and would pervert the gospel of Christ.*

This is very important, pay close attention, Paul is speaking about the Great Falling Away and who will be doing the false teaching;

> *8 But though we, or an Angel from heaven, preach any other gospel unto you than that which we have preached unto you, let him be accursed.*

No matter if it is a human false teacher/preacher or if it is an angel from heaven such as Satan himself don't be a part of their church! It may cost you your eternal soul! In the fourth chapter of 2 Timothy, Paul gives a final warning:

> *3 For the time will come when they will not endure sound doctrine; but after their own lusts shall they keep to themselves teachers, having itching ears;*
>
> *4 And they shall turn away their ears from the truth and shall be turned unto fables.*

He is coming. And he's going to be beautiful, he's going to be powerful, and most of the world will follow him. What does *itching* ears mean in verse 3 that describes the false earthly teachers the False Savior will employ, after they abandon *sound doctrine*? It will be ears that need to be scratched by flattery and lies. Do you remember what Satan's sin was against God? It was pride, in the First Earth Age, Satan believed he was greater than God and engineered a rebellion. He lost his battle with God, but his sin will be the same in the Last Days just as Daniel described, he will sit in the Holy Place convincing himself he is God. Will he convince you? Will you follow him because he flatters you and tells you the lies you want to hear? Be very careful, he will use your pride against you, and his goal is to have you worship him as God.

I bet if I asked you to recite the First Commandment you wouldn't have a problem. *Thou shalt have no other gods before me* (Ex. 20:3). I remember it from my early Catechism classes; you probably remember it also from your earliest teachings in Christianity, no matter what denomination you might have embraced, past or present. This is the number one thing God does not want us to do, and yet looking back through the Old Testament, it was the one sin God's people always seemed to fall into. It brought them grief, plagues, and caused them to be scattered across the globe. Even Solomon, with all his wisdom, in the end was seduced into worshiping the false gods and idols of his many foreign wives. It will be the Great Temptation leading to the greatest sin of this Second Earth Age; Satan himself, as Antichrist, will be worshiped as God by many.

This is the Great Deception of the End Times, this is the lie that will lead to the Great Falling Away. Will you be deceived? Will you be taken in by the Babylon of the End Times? The word Babylon itself means confusion, the Confusion of the End Times. Look around, what do you see going on in the world today? What have you seen happening to the world, especially over the past few years? Everything that was normal is now abnormal. Everything that was acceptable is now unacceptable.

We're supposed to allow males to use female bathrooms because they identify as female that day. We're supposed to give up all the rights of American citizens to illegal aliens who have entered this country by breaking our laws. We have American-born citizens living in poverty and yet we're supposed to pay for the medical and educational expenses of illegal aliens in this country. In parts of this country people pay as much as five dollars for a cup of coffee. Kids are paying one hundred to two hundred dollars and sometimes more for a pair of sneakers. Athletes making millions of dollars a year playing football kneel at the playing of our National Anthem even though they are unable to explain what they are protesting, while their activity is driving viewers away from their sport by the millions.

Students protest the right of free speech on college campuses, and demand safe spaces to protect them from speech that is frightening. At the same time, tenured professors at respected universities encourage students to riot, and rant and rave about how evil their opposition is. Hollywood makes movies about how to assassinate presidents they don't like; at the same time, they promote the confiscation of all guns from the American people.

One of the world's most recognized and decorated male athletes of all time becomes a reality TV star, and then tells the world he is now a woman. Boys that have determined they should have been born girls can participate in athletic events against the opposite sex. One such boy, Mack Beggs, on February 24, 2017, in Cypress, Texas, completed an undefeated season by winning a controversial Texas state girl's wrestling title.

Homosexuality has been normalized. I challenge you to find a primetime TV program, comedy or drama that doesn't feature at least one homosexual character. I'm sure there are some, but they are far and few between. Sodomy, which has always been considered illegal in the past, has been normalized, and even presented as acceptable to our young children. On June 29, 2013, the *New Yorker* featured Sesame Street characters as gay on their front cover, and on June 26, 2017 the iconic children's show, *Sesame Street*, announced its support for the LGBT movement. Bert and Ernie were created to teach pre-schoolers that people can be good friends with those who are very different from themselves promoting the importance of diversity. But now, Burt and Ernie have been kidnapped by progressives, and a huge push from the liberal left to officially announce their "gayness" continues. And now, there is a push in the California public school system to teach sexual orientation to children as young as five and six years old.

Teachers, coaches, and other school employees are having sexual relationships with their students at an ever-accelerating rate. Trust in this nation's educators has been eroding away for years. Larry Nassar, team doctor for USA women's gymnastics team has been accused by more than 125 women of allegedly sexually assaulting them under the pretense of medical treatment. This went unreported for years, recently two-time Olympic medalist McKayla Maroney revealed Nassar abused her for seven years, starting when she was only thirteen years old. Jerry Sandusky, an assistant coach for the Penn State football team was convicted on June 22, 2012, of forty-five counts of sexual abuse against members of the Nittany Lions football team. These abuses occurred between 1994 and 2009, for almost fifteen years, without being reported.

At this time, over fifty teachers have been caught, prosecuted, and/or convicted of having extracurricular activities with their students. One teacher, Brianna Altice, a teacher at Davis High School in Utah, was arrested in 2013 for having a sexual relationship with one of her sixteen-year-old students. After charges were filed it was discovered Brianna was having a sexual relationship with two more of her students at the same time. More recently Sarah Jones, a former Bengals' cheerleader now teacher, was having a sexual relationship with a seventeen-year-old student at the high school where she taught. Jones has now divorced her husband and is engaged to her former student. It has been rumored that she is now getting her own reality TV show.

Preachers are not immune to the Confusion of Babylon, consider Jimmy Swaggart, James and Tammy Faye Baker, along with several others, and the entire Roman Catholic Church's clergy that have been involved in child abuse scandals. Sex scandals are everywhere within the ecumenical world and have been since the early days of the Church. Only the most famous participants usually come to light on a national basis, but anyone who has gone to church for very long, no matter what denomination, is sure to have heard of a scandal or two of this type. In 1976, the Episcopal Church, declared that homosexual persons have a full and equal claim along with other persons of faith, to the promises of the Bible. This somehow insinuates that there is no sin involved with homosexuality. In 2003, the first openly gay bishop was ordained and then in 2015 the Episcopal Church began to recognize and make available the right of marriage to all people regardless of gender. It seems that in every religious cult that has been exposed over this past century, some type of sexual activity or misconduct has been involved. In most instances, in some way, shape or form, sex is used to influence and control other members of the cult.

Politicians also have a long history in this country of participating in what eventually leads to sexual scandals. Many will tell you there is a fine line between religion and politics, Bill Clinton is perhaps the most famous of all politicians engaging in illicit sexual activity, but he is only the tip of the iceberg. These are the people we are supposed to trust the most; ministers and politicians. These are the people that we trust as a nation to guard our spiritual and political rights. Confusion abounds.

CHAPTER 15

The Four Hidden Dynasties

The things that are going on in the world today are not normal; to the contrary, they are far from normal. Our educational systems have collapsed into institutions that push unproven theories, promote political agendas, produce abnormal behaviors, and neglect the subjects that have been traditional educational basics for thousands of years. As tuition for a higher education increases every year, the advantages of graduating from these institutions of higher learning are steeply declining. We have been told since we were children that a higher education is the key to a better life that's not necessarily true anymore. A certified welder in today's economy will, in many cases, make more than a person working in fields that require a college degree. Education is one of the four Hidden Dynasties that will be used to deceive God's children in the End Times. This indoctrination has been happening for many years; I experienced it firsthand in the 1970s.

Science is a part of higher education and continues to support unsubstantiated theories and claims about everything from the origin of life to global warming. They disregard pertinent data, and sometimes even make up their own to bolster their unprovable theories. Higher education has been running interference for science for decades, humiliating and belittling any student that believes anything outside their doctrine, especially Christianity. Espousing theories such as evolution that cannot be proven and which continue to unravel daily with each new discovery.

Politics is another of the four Hidden Dynasties; the governments of the world will support and help successfully usher in the false Messiah. Politics uses the Hidden Dynasty of Education through science; if you have the money to offer a research grant on any subject, you can have studies done to prove just about anything you want, and then those findings are used for political purposes. The first thing anyone should do before believing any scientific study these days is to see who paid for the study. When the time comes, the political powers of this global world, along with the global scientific community, and the institutions of higher education worldwide will back the Antichrist.

Those that control the Hidden Dynasty of the Economy have a goal in mind for all of humanity and it involves keeping them poor and under control. These powerful people will happily support the Antichrist if it means it will keep the status quo. They will dictate when you can buy and when you can sell, and through regulations of the Political Dynasty they will control the economy. It is made clear in the Book of Amos that God is going to put holes in the pockets of his unbelieving children, and the Hidden Dynasty of the Economy plays a part. In chapter 8 God states,

> *4 Hear this, O ye that swallow up the needy, even to make the poor of the land fail,*

> *5 Saying, when will the new moon be gone, that we may sell corn? And the Sabbath, that we may set forth wheat, making the ephah small, and the shekel great, and falsifying the balances by deceit?*

At this time, an *ephah* was worth more than a *shekel*, they are going to turn things upside down. And what is meant by *balances* in this verse? *Balances* in this verse is Strong's word number 3976 and means *a set of scales*. So according to this verse the scales used to keep people honest are going to be tampered with and through deceit the people will be cheated and kept poor.

*6 That we may buy the poor for silver, and the needy
for a pair of shoes; yea, and sell the refuse of the wheat?*

There are many names for these people, but I think the one we hear the most today is Globalists. These powerful controllers of the Hidden Dynasty of the Economy, and those of the Hidden Dynasty of Education will team up with those of the Hidden Dynasty of Politics, and with the help of the media will support the False Christ. You have probably heard the old saying: "follow the money," that has never been truer than in the Confusion of the End Times. The rich will control the poor and will bring ruin upon the people. Then just as it says in Daniel, when Antichrist arrives peacefully and prosperously, offering to save mankind from this terrible situation, he will be embraced and will receive the backing of the Hidden Dynasties. Satan, pretending to be the Savior returned, will be embraced by the same people that brought on the poverty and pain in the first place.

So we have the Hidden Dynasties of Education, Economics, and Politics, working together to usher in and support the false Messiah, but what is the Fourth Hidden Dynasty? In many ways it is the most powerful of all and will be an instrumental tool of Satan in deceiving the world. Amos chapter 8 states,

> *11 Behold, the days come, saith the Lord God, that
> I will send a famine in the land, not a famine of
> bread, nor a thirst for water, but of hearing the
> words of the Lord:*
>
> *12 And they shall wander from sea to sea, and from
> the north even to the east, they shall run to and fro
> to seek the word of the Lord and shall not find it.*

The Fourth Hidden Dynasty is Religion, and I believe it will be the most devastating to Christians of all the Hidden Dynasties. This brings us to an intriguing and puzzling question that I grappled with for years:

*What lie could fool good churchgoing Christians, in
fact entire congregations and whole denominations,
along with all the other religions of the world, and
cause them all to be taken in by this fake?*

What New Religion, what New Doctrine, could be so powerful that it would fool the entire world? We can see this famine for the word of God today, look anywhere, any denomination you want to choose, you will see the famine. Watch most television evangelists and preachers, and you will see one or two lines of Scripture presented, and then an hour of preaching about stuff and things. This bloviating does not necessarily have anything to do with the word of God, and many times draws false conclusions and spreads false teaching throughout the Christian world. There is so much false teaching out there today it is breath taking. My rule of thumb is, if you can't find it in the Bible, then it is nothing more than something cooked up in some person's head. Jesus told us in the Book of Mark chapter 13, verse 23, that He has told us all things. If you can't find it in the Holy Bible, and I would insist the King James Version, then don't believe it as GOSPEL!

One of the greatest modern-day examples of false teaching is the Rapture Theory, which was never taught until around the year 1830, and has no basis in Scripture except those invented in the minds of men. The word rapture is never mentioned in the Bible, and the one place where Paul speaks of being caught up with the Lord takes place at Christ's return. At the TRUE Christ's return, not at or before the appearance of the FALSE Messiah. In many places in the Bible we are told to stand our ground against Satan. In Ephesians we are told to put on the Gospel Armor to do battle with Satan when he returns, and yet these false teachers feed the flock lies. Beware, the confusion of Babylon of the End Times is here.

Religious leaders will flock to the false Messiah and accept him as their Lord and Savior bringing many if not of all their congregations with them. This is a very treacherous time for Christians, are you prepared for it? Still the question remains, what New Religion, or New Doctrine could be so dynamic and powerful that it could bring the entire world to its knees before this fake?

It will be the greatest revival of all times, Science will back him with all their scientific data. Political governments all over the world will back him, world religions and their leaders will flock to him, because he will give them power over their constituents and congregations. And the economic powers of the world will back him too, because he will make them rich. But what about you what's going to convince you? Will you be the little lamb that follows your religious leader into a New Religion? Or will you be so convinced that he will pay your bills and take care of all your earthly needs and desires forever that you will bow down and worship him?

Some people will sell out for power, some people will sell out for money, and others will be so deceived they will just believe, because there is a famine in the world today for hearing the word of God. Bible illiteracy abounds in this country today, and indeed throughout the entire world. Everywhere you look, you find false teaching in Christianity. Some preachers tell you you must go through them to get to God for everything; they say, "Send me money, and I'll pray to Him for you." Some say you must confess to him, or her, or them, to have your sins forgiven. Some say you have to pay them money or you will lose the blessings of God. Some say you don't have to worry at all, that God loves all his children and He will never bring judgement and correction to the world. Some say; don't worry you're not going to be here, we are going to fly away. Or others tell you; if you haven't been baptized by our church you are going to burn in the hell. They're all lies; they are part of the Confusion. How many preachers or teachers have told you the false Christ comes first? Believe me, God doesn't like any of it, He is not happy about the false teachers. In the Book of Amos chapter 5, God is talking to the false teachers;

21 I hate, I despise your feast days, and I will not smell in your solemn assemblies

22 Though you offer me burnt offerings and your meat offerings, I will not accept them: neither will I regard the peace offerings of your fat beasts.

God doesn't want anything to do with the false teachers and their lies, He certainly is not going to bless them. In verse 21 the word *smell* is Strong's number 7308, *ruwach* in the Hebrew, which as a noun means *mind, spirit, wind.* We use the word when we speak of the Holy Spirit; the holy Ruwach. So what God is telling these phonies is the Holy Spirit is not going to be part of their assemblies/churches, He doesn't want their offerings, He doesn't want anything they have.

> *23 Take thou away from me the noise of the songs;*
> *for I will not hear the melody of thy viols.*

No, God doesn't like it at all, he gave us the First Commandment and it is our job to follow it. If we don't we will pay the price. So don't be deceived, false teachers are everywhere. Even if modern-day science backs up the claims of this false Christ, you must not believe them. If every day on the television, you are told that this or that is true, but it goes against God's teachings do not waver. It's going to be difficult, you have been told this in the scriptures, but if you ask for strength from God to make it through this trying time God promises, you will be delivered.

Personally, I have lived in the academic world, on and off, for over fifty years, as a student and then as a professor. I can testify, Higher Education is infested with Confusion, the deception never ends. A few years ago, when I was the director for an Arizona community college, I hired a highly qualified Christian man to teach the sciences on our campus. He was under fire almost immediately by the head of his department, who is said to be a practicing Catholic, because he taught evolution was a theory not a law of science. I began monitoring his class because I knew someday I would either be required to speak against him or defend him for what he was teaching in the classroom. The professor taught his students that evolution is a theory, just as is creation. The professor taught that unless you could absolutely prove something through repeated experimentation it was not a Law. He taught that unless the results were ALWAYS the same it was nothing more than a theory, which means it is not provable. He was absolutely correct. This professor was run out of this particular "Institution of Higher Learning" shortly after I retired, even though he had some of the highest ratings from students of any professor working at the college. Confusion prevailed.

Shortly after I retired, I worked for the only American university in Central America helping to facilitate their transition into controlling the campus they had just purchased in Nicaragua. I ended up teaching at the university my last year in Nicaragua and got to know several of the university's professors. One of my favorite instructors was the Biology professor, and I was able to have several revealing conversations with him concerning evolution. While he would admit there was no real scientific proof of the evolution of one species into another, he believed it wholeheartedly because it was what he was taught in school. Upon questioning him about skeletal evidence, or the lack of it, he would retreat into his comfortable place of just believing in evolution. What amazed me most was he too was a devout Catholic and struggled continually with the issue of creation. His answer, as I think is true with many Christian scientists, was that God could create the universe any way He wanted even through evolution. I would always ask; but where's the proof? Where is the skeletal evidence of any transition from one species to another? Where is the skeleton of a fish changing into a bird, or a monkey changing into a human? I would say to him: "If evolution is a never-ending process as Darwin claimed, shouldn't we be able to see species changing right before our eyes?" He had no answers to these questions because there are none. Confusion, confusion, confusion, it is everywhere we look. Even as discoveries in genetics prove it is impossible that mankind evolved from the apes, the scientists hold on to their old sacred beliefs.

Less than five hundred years ago Science told us the world was flat and that if we sailed to the end of the earth we would fall off into some unknown abyss. People were persecuted and killed for disagreeing with this "scientific fact" and the people believed. It is the same attitude of supremacy we see today by the scientific community that allows the media to condemn anyone who disagrees with them. Even though it's been proven that the scientific community has cherry picked figures, and in some cases made the data up to support their theories, the media is right there backing their lies and spreading their venom. Mass media of today is one of the arms of the Four Hidden Dynasties and they use it to spread the deception.

CHAPTER 16

The Deadly Wound

 One of the most mysterious prophecies about the End Times concerns the seven-headed beast with ten horns adorned with ten crowns which rose out of the sea and is found in the Book of Revelation. One of the beast's heads is **wounded to death**, and then is healed through the power of the dragon. Revelation 13:

> *1 And I stood upon the sand of the sea, and saw a beast rise up out of the sea, having seven heads and ten horns, and upon his horns ten crowns, and upon his heads the name of blasphemy.*

In Bible prophecy, whenever the *sea* is referenced it refers to the people of the world. Whenever *horns* are referenced it refers to power, and whenever *crowns* are referenced it refers to rulership. *Blasphemy* is speaking against God, denying or diminishing His sovereignty.

> *2 And the beast which I saw was like unto a leopard, and his feet were as the feet of a bear, and the mouth as the mouth of a lion: and the dragon gave him his power; and his seat, and great authority.*

First, we must agree that there is no such thing as a seven headed beast, so open your mind to God's truth. Every time some unworldly example, such as a seven-headed beast, is used in Bible prophecy it refers to the formation of some type of organizational or governmental structure. The references in this verse to a leopard, bear, and lion are significant, because these are the first three beasts of Daniel's dream in the Book of Daniel chapter 7. These *three beasts* of Daniel refer to the three all-powerful world governmental structures that existed in the past, preceding the one world empire of the End Times, which is yet to come. The fourth beast Daniel sees in the seventh chapter is the seven headed beast of Revelation that will receive a *deadly wound*. A lion's mouth is known for its strength and how it rips and tears its pry apart, it is an attitude. The bear is known as a symbol of Russia and the leopard is the symbol of the hidden nation that changes their spots; the Kenites. I hope you are aware of who the *dragon* is, he controls the fourth beast or governmental structure and all the components from the first three beasts of Daniel, which are going to be present in the fourth. Satan gives this organization a *seat* (Strong's number 2362 in the Greek, means *power, a throne*) and *great authority* over the world.

> *3 And I saw one of his heads as it were wounded to death: and his deadly wound was healed: and all the world wondered after the beast.*

How does an organization receive a *deadly wound?* One way would be by having one or two of its biggest most powerful members leave the organization, and you could heal it by bringing that member back into the organization...or by destroying that member.

> *4 And they worshipped the dragon which gave power unto the beast: and they worshipped the beast saying, who is like unto the beast? Who is able to make war with him?*

If you look at the world situation today, you can see the possible development of a One World System taking place. You have the European Union, with or without Great Britain. You have Russia, or Rush as it is called in the Bible, who are the descendants of Esau.

You have Central and South America, predominantly Christian countries, leaning farther and farther toward socialism. Confusion is everywhere. You have China and Japan living in the same region espousing totally different political beliefs, both threatened by the insanity that has plagued them, called North Korea. You have South Korea, a prosperous democratic nation continually threatened by its neighbor to the north. There are the countries of the African continent including Egypt, and we can't forget Iran and Syria, and others continually pushing the envelope in the Middle East. You have the United States and Israel, who have been committed to world peace and the spread of democracy since the end of World War II, and the Kenites are mixed in everywhere. All these divergent forces are loosely held together by the United Nations.

The world is in turmoil, countries being run by crazy dictators, others run by power-hungry aristocrats. The Book of Revelation tells us the Beast, will almost achieve world peace. But something happens, the *deadly wound* occurs, the controlling world organization that Daniel calls the *fourth beast* fails at first. Then, Satan steps in.

We are currently watching the results of the United States government negotiating with other countries to achieve world peace. For the past several years, we have witnessed our government make concessions to countries that would be unimaginable twenty or thirty years ago. Recently, by playing hardball and refusing to knuckle under to pressure from other countries, it seems we are looking out for our own interests more than others these days. It's easy to envision a situation and time where our country or one of our allies would walk away from the negotiating table because of an unwillingness to accept an agreement or treaty detrimental to our country or our allies, or one that is so egregiously foul it can't be tolerated. Hence a deadly wound.

Don't misunderstand. I'm not saying this is how it will transpire. I haven't received some secret message on the matter. But there are only so many scenarios that will fit the prophecies of the End Times, we owe it to ourselves to explore them, so we are not deceived. And as I said earlier, the question that needs to be asked is what lie, what new religion, what new piece of false information could fool the entire world, especially Christians, into worshiping Satan? Examination of different scenarios of what could possibly happen hopefully will start the thought process in some and make the point that something is going to happen to fulfill these prophecies. I don't believe it's that far away, remember the Parable of the Fig Tree. Although I don't know exactly what will cause the deadly wound, I do know it will involve world peace and will trigger the appearance of Instead of Christ on earth. How do I know this? Jeremiah, chapter 6 warns us of this time:

> *13 For from the least of them even unto the greatest of them everyone is given to covetousness; and from the prophet even unto the priest everyone dealth falsely.*

> *14 They have healed also the hurt of the daughter of my people slightly, saying, Peace, peace; when there is no peace.*

It is not going to be pretty, he wants your soul, and you won't be able to trust anyone. At the same time, they will try to whitewash the sins being committed, they will lie to the people claiming there is peace when there is none. And in the book of Matthew chapter 24, Christ warns us,

> *6 And you shall hear of wars and rumors of wars: see that ye be not troubled: for all these things must come to pass, but the end is not yet.*

> *7 For nation shall rise against nation, and kingdom against kingdom: and there shall be famines, and pestilence, and earthquakes in divers places.*

We've seen all these things of course, but we haven't seen the peace, peace, peace. It could be right around the corner, but when it happens, you'll know it, if you're familiar with God's word. It might not happen exactly how you envision it, but when you see the supernatural being along with all his lieutenants come to earth, claiming to have all the answers, in fact claiming to be God the creator, you will recognize them if you know the truth. Just remember, the false Messiah comes first. Satan comes at the sixth trump; the true Messiah comes at the seventh trump. Six comes before seven, it's just that simple, don't be deceived. Remember, Paul says in 2 Thessalonians chapter 2:

> *3 Let no man deceive you by any means: for that day shall not come, except there come a falling away first, and that man of sin be revealed, the son of perdition,*
>
> *4 Who opposeth and exalteth himself above all that is called God, and that is worshiped; so that he as God sitteth in the temple of God, shewing himself that he is God.*

The false Christ comes first, not after Jesus returns… FIRST!

CHAPTER 17

The Greatest Revival
of All Time

Picture this, Satan comes to Earth, he is beautiful, probably looks a lot like how you picture Jesus. In the twenty-eighth chapter of Ezekiel, verse 12 God says Satan is *perfect in beauty*. And he is powerful; he has supernatural powers no one has seen since Christ walked the earth. Remember God was so concerned about the power of Satan and the weakness of His children, that He shortened the days Satan will be on earth. This isn't going to be any ordinary revival, this really is going to be the Greatest Show on Earth. Imagine, Satan and his lieutenants, supernatural beings presenting themselves to the world as Jesus returning with his army of angels. Or perhaps, Satan will have some other story. Science will back the story no matter what; science will probably even offer data and statistics to prove he is God. The governments of the world will pledge allegiance to him, higher education will handle his appearance as proof that they have been right all along about Christianity. Christianity will be discarded for the New Religion of the false Messiah, perhaps even outlawed. His message will be spread worldwide, probably televised worldwide. He will bring new and amazing things, perhaps technology that will impress and amaze the people. Read the accounts of the false Messiah in the New Testament, there is no doubt that Satan will exercise his supernatural power in his attempt to prove he is God. It will be a revival like no other, the Greatest Show on Earth!

There may not be a revival tent, but the Greatest Show on Earth will be brought to the people of earth by supernatural beings from another dimension. It's what the Bible tells us is going to happen, he will be selling his snake oil to whoever is buying. In the thirteenth chapter of Revelation, just before a successful One World System is a reality, something happens, and it falls apart, the failure of the One World System signals Satan's banishment to earth. He will bring unity to the One World System and heal the Deadly Wound. Then, as we are told in Daniel, he will be magnificent, peaceful, and bring prosperity to those that worship him. Imagine the show he will put on; healings, supernatural demonstrations of power, perhaps even what appears to be raising the dead. And remember, Matthew 24,

> *10 And then shall many be offended, and shall betray one another, and shall hate one another.*

And in Mark chapter 13,

> *12 Now the brother shall betray brother to death, and the father the son; and children shall rise up against their parents, and shall cause them to be put to death.*

This is important for the elect! Remember according to God Himself, not one hair on your head will be harmed by Satan, so what does this verse mean? *Death* is one of Satan's names, Hebrews 2:14, and many that are brought up to him will embrace him, they will embrace *death*. When you, as one of God's elect, are given up to *death*, you will testify. You will give yourself over to the Holy Spirit and allow Him to testify the truth of God through you. You will be on the main stage of the Greatest Show on Earth; the Greatest Revival of All Time, and you are going to be the show-stopper.

The proceedings no doubt, will be televised worldwide. Satan's wondrous feats will be reported by the world's major newspapers and on TV and radio everywhere. Christians will flock to him by the millions; some will be brought by their religious leaders. Millions more will be brought into his New Religion by conversion from their prior beliefs. The new converts' job will be simple; bring their friends and family into the flock. The possibilities of his promises are unlimited, he won't ever have to make good on most of them. Remember, he has only a short period of time here on earth, so he will be able to promise anything that happens in the future without ever having to deliver.

Hold on to your seat, the greatest show on earth is coming to your town. It will be a star-studded affair, some of the biggest names and some of the most important people on earth will be part of the show. World leaders from every corner of the globe will come to support him; the hidden Dynasty of the Economy will be in full gear supporting the false Messiah. Great world scholars and renowned scientists will come to pay homage to him and throw the support of the entire world scientific community behind him, and his story. World religious leaders will come to his throne and bow before him, even Iran's Ayatollah. The evangelists, preachers, and reverends from all Christian denominations will come and convert to his New Religion, some bringing entire congregations with them.

He will use Bible scripture in his false narrative, it is his MO; he's a Scripture lawyer. He knows Scripture better than most of us and he will use it in his deception. Look at the temptation of Christ, how did Satan do it? He tempted Christ through Bible scripture, twisting it just a little, changing the context slightly. Are you sharp enough to catch his deception? Matthew chapter 4:

> *5 Then the devil taketh Him up into the holy city, and said to Him on a pinnacle of the Temple,*
>
> *6 And (Satan) saith unto Him, if thou be the Son of God, cast thyself down: for it is written, He shall give His angels charge concerning thee: and in their hands they shall bear thee up, lest at any time thou dash thy foot against a stone.*

Without looking it up, do you know how he twisted the Scripture? It sounds right but the changes are subtle. Satan was supposedly quoting from Psalms 91:

> *10 There shall no evil befall thee, neither shall any plague come nigh thy dwelling.*
>
> *11 For he shall give his angels charge over thee, to keep thee in all thy ways.*
>
> *12 They shall bear thee up in their hands, lest thou dash thy foot against a stone.*

Do you see the lie? Do you see how Satan changed the Scripture? The angels are charged to make sure Christ keeps to all of God's ways. This was an attempt upon Jesus's life! Satan knew that if Christ cast Himself down pridefully thinking God would protect Him because He was so great, it would be a sin and the sin would make Him imperfect. It would be the end of Messiah; He would be imperfect and unworthy to redeem our sins. He would become an imperfect offering for the sins of the world that God could not accept. Satan appealed to Christ's pride, the same weakness Satan succumbed to in the First Earth Age. But Jesus Christ, the Son of God, is perfect and was not fooled by Satan's lies. Satan first tempted Christ through his fleshly needs, remember Jesus had been in the desert for forty days. Satan offered him food, but Christ rebuffed Satan's temptations. Satan's third and final temptation was for power, Satan offered Jesus the power and glory of all the greatest kingdoms on earth. It was Satan's to give; Satan is the Prince of this World during this Earth Age. But Christ was not tempted, and ordered Satan behind Him, where he remains until this day.

It is important to know what Satan used in his temptations of Christ because he will tempt us in the same manner. His attack was three-prong; desires of the flesh, pride supported by Scripture, and the desire for power and glory. Satan hasn't changed, he is the same lying deceiver that tempted Christ, just like he tempted Adam and

Eve in the Garden. It will be the same again when he returns the next time, we all need to be ready for it. The false Messiah will lie to us using Scripture, but it will be a little twisted and changed. He will appeal to our physical needs and desires, he and his fallen angels are very attracted to humans, remember according to Genesis they wed the daughters of Adam and had children with them. Satan and his crew are desirous of human fleshly things, consider what happened to Adam and Eve in the Garden. He will appeal to our ego, stoking the fire of human pride. He will offer things that will make life easier; he will offer other things, power and glory. It's going to be the Greatest Show on Earth and the greatest temptation of all time, and the elect will be on center stage. The confusion, the lies, the excitement, the danger; the Greatest Revival of All Time is coming.

God will not leave us alone at this time, in addition to the Holy Spirit, He is sending His Two Witnesses. In Revelation chapter 11, God tells us,

> *3 And I will give power unto my two witnesses, and they shall prophesy a thousand two hundred and threescore days clothed in sackcloth.*

> *4 These are the two olive trees, and the two candlesticks (lampstands in Zechariah chapter 4) standing before the God of the earth.*

They will be here giving us support through the Holy Spirit, delivering the oil of truth to God's children. The Bible says they will be here 1,260 days, which just happens to be three and one-half years and is also about ten days longer than the original time Satan was to be loosed on the world. Remember Satan was to be here forty-two months, before the time was shortened. All prophecies about Satan are in months or moons and have to do with darkness and deceit. All prophecies about Christ are in days and have to do with the light and truth. Forty-two months is about ten days less than the time the Two Witnesses will be here. Scripture says they will be clothed in sackcloth which means they'll be repenting for the sins of the world and preaching repentance to God's children. The two witnesses are the two olive trees and the two lampstands of Zachariah's vision in chapter 4, and this Scripture speaks of how there are seven lamps connected to each of the olive trees. They are connected by golden pipes and through the pipes the oil of truth will flow. Zachariah chapter 4:

> *11 Then answered I, and said unto him, what are these two olive trees upon the right side of the candlestick and upon the left side thereof?*
>
> *12 And I answered again, and said unto him, what be these two olive branches which through the two golden pipes empty the golden oil out of themselves?*
>
> *13 And he answered me and said, knowest thou not what these be? And I said, No, my lord.*
>
> *14 Then said he, these are the two anointed ones, that stand by the Lord of the whole earth.*

We will have the Two Witnesses with us for support. The time Satan will be allowed on earth has been shortened according to the Books of Matthew and Mark, so certainly the time the Two Witnesses will be here has been shortened proportionately. The Greatest Revival of All Time will be going on nonstop; the Two Witnesses will be prophesying the Word of God and speaking the truth. As Jesus told us, all things have been revealed, so their prophecies will naturally align with what the Word has already told us. They will be our lifeline; their truth will be the oil that flows into God's elect, who become the lamps of light at the time of total darkness. The midnight hour will be upon us. And the Great Revival will continue, day and night, twenty-four hours a day, every channel on your TV will be showing it. Today, when a shooting takes place, or a bridge collapses, or a major storm is approaching our coast, there is twenty-four seven, bumper-to-bumper, exclusive news coverage across the world. Imagine the intensity of the coverage that will take place when the false Messiah arrives.

It will be an alarming and stressful time, especially for those caught off guard. Many Christians believe that if the Book of Revelation is true, these events will take place far in the future. Nonbelievers are much more worried about things like the long-term effects of global warming and they think the whole Antichrist story is fantasy. Both these groups are going to be easy pickings for the false Messiah; they will flock to him by the millions. Things will go very good for the Antichrist in the beginning but that will not last long. When things begin to turn against him and his angels, his followers are likely to become more and more agitated. It won't take long for them to identify who is with them and everyone else will be a target for conversion. As events escalate on the world stage the false Messiah will be backed further and further into a corner, then the trials and testimonies will begin. The elect will be the only ones left that have not publicly embraced Satan as their Lord and Savior, and they will be delivered up to *Death* himself, *Lucifer*, the *Destroyer*, the *Serpent*. These are all different names found for Satan in the Bible, but they all refer to the same guy; the *devil*.

So here we are at the crossroads, Angels or Aliens? As I said in the beginning, I agree with much of what the ANCIENT ASTRONAUT THEORISTS have presented over the last twenty years. They have shined a light on physical evidence remaining on this planet that proves, beyond a shadow of a doubt in my opinion; intelligent life with advanced technology inhabited this planet long before humans did. ANCIENT ASTRONAUT THEORISTS are mistaken, however, in their use of the term extraterrestrial rather than supernatural, when referring to these beings that inhabited earth long ago. I also believe the ANCIENT ASTRONAUT THEORISTS are being used by the Four Hidden Dynasties to further the new lie against Creation. What has happened is, through the success of science fiction books, movies, and TV programs, a large portion of the population now believe in the existence of extraterrestrial beings from outer space. The idea of a race of people from another planet coming to earth and beginning a new life form is the foundation of the beliefs and theories offered to us by the ANCIENT ASTRONAUT THEORISTS. So let's take this theory and play it out, but according to my definition of who is piloting these UFOs. Again, I'm not saying this is what's going to happen, I have no inside information other than what the Bible teaches us. The name of my story might be the *Alien Invasion*, or perhaps *Father Returns.*

PART FOUR

THE ALIEN INVASION

CHAPTER 18

The Spring

May 1
Sometime in the Future

The United States Congress had allowed spending to grow unchecked for years, and the Federal Reserve had been manipulating monetary policy and interest rates in America for decades. Debt had accelerated out of control and, the debt of the government wasn't the only thing out of control, personal debt in America had grown to a record level. Foreign debt was worse and was not going to change under the current circumstances. When the worldwide economic bubble burst, the World Peace Conference fell apart.

Now, a fleet of unidentified flying objects was hovering over every major city of the world including Moscow, Beijing, Tehran, Jerusalem, and Washington, DC. In expected human fashion, the world's forces of evil aimed their most powerful weapons at these unusual flying objects. When after a week there was no response to numerous attempts to communicate with them, by Russian and Chinese negotiators for the UN, the world's forces of destruction were poised to attack. These amber colored saucers, however, seemed to simply be watching the inhabitants of earth. Then suddenly, Su-57 fighter jets began to fire missile after missile at the unidentified flying objects hovering over Moscow, the barrage over the Homeland was intense.

The same thing was happening over other cities including Beijing, Tehran, and Damascus. The attacks continued for over twenty minutes involving the air forces of several nations in the Middle East, Africa, and Europe. Billions of dollars of high-tech weaponry was unleashed on the uninvited visitors, as the world watched in horror with dark expectations. People fled to bomb shelters and other protected areas worldwide expecting the worst, but the deadly high-tech missiles just bounced off some type of shield around the crafts like toothpicks being tossed against a stone wall.

Just days earlier, the world had been brought to the brink of global peace, only to have those hopes dashed to pieces due to the withdrawal of two major players in the world alliance. Nations were in an upheaval with entire economies imploding, the explosion of inflation worldwide drove prices of everything through the roof. If people had the money to buy food, the shelves were empty. The images of rioting people worldwide filled every TV screen, world leaders were ready to throw away everything, itching to attack their enemies, World War III seemed unavoidable. Then suddenly these whirling metal discs appeared above capitals across the globe, silently observing. Now, the world's most powerful weapons were being thrown at these unannounced visitors. Without any provocation these visitors from another…place were treated as mortal enemies, and only a few voices worldwide had called for restraint and patience. These were the same voices that were blamed for the collapse of the World Governments' peace program, and now they were ignored again.

Congregations around the world, of all different faiths and beliefs came together to pray. The telephone systems worldwide were jammed, and on the verge of collapse. Children in schools all around the world climbed under desks in some imaginary attempt to protect themselves from the coming nuclear onslaught. Mass transit of all kinds worldwide was pressed to the point of breakdown. Air flights were canceled across the globe, no one could go home, they were stuck in what they perceived to be the crosshairs of alien invaders. The Vatican announced an hour of prayer to begin immediately, asking God for protection. Around the time it became absolutely clear no weapon of destruction in the possession of mankind could do anything to one of these ships, the human race received their first communication from the visitors. The communication came in the form of a video feed that over took every video screen in the world at the same instant. Televisions, computer screens, telephones, every screen connected to a network across the globe displayed the video feed from the aliens.

The screens flickered, and the flight deck of the alien mothership came into view, and the world was given its first look at the alien beings. They didn't look anything like you would expect, they weren't small, and gray, with big globe looking eyes and they weren't green with reptile skin; they looked like regular handsome young men! In fact, the commander, who was obviously in total control, was beautifully handsome, with long flowing hair, and he wore flowing robes of royal purple, trimmed in fine gold. He looked about thirty but his movements communicated maturity and understanding of things mysterious and old. His crew members were all about the same age, they looked to be in their twenties or thirties, handsome, and all looked to be male. The interior of the craft and the flight deck didn't look like what you might expect either. There were no switches or blinking lights, there wasn't any levers to pull or buttons to push, the only stationary things in view were the chairs in which the crew sat, and of course the throne. The commander with flowing hair, sat on what appeared to be a solid gold throne with the six crew members sitting in a circle around him. The crew members were also in robes, but not of purple, they were long and flowing and black.

The magnificent glowing commander with flowing long hair held up his hand, in what seemed to be a greeting, and began to speak. His expression was relaxed and kind; it gave the listener a feeling of security. His eyes were intense and cast an aura of deep understanding; they were dark brown and piercing. His words were translated by experts into every language of the world and then flooded the ears of his listeners like honey flowing into the buds of their minds, calmness and perceived understanding exploded in their minds. All those that heard the message felt the same super intensive sensation, it was like a supernova exploded in their minds and they suddenly believed they understood everything the glorious being was saying and the meaning of it. The listeners were convinced of the truth of his message and marveled at the simplicity and beauty of the message. As if they were in a trance, their physical responses were in unison, their smiles, their heads nodding, the glazed expression in their eyes.

"My children," the beautiful extraterrestrial began, "we mean you no harm. We are here to help you, we love you, do not be afraid. We know what you're going through my children, we understand everything. We have many things to share with you, things you cannot even imagine yet. We will teach you things and explain the deepest secrets of mankind. You must trust us now, this display of mistrust you have shown us by this unwarranted attack hurts us deeply. You are part of us, we are part of you, we cannot be separated." Crowds around the world were glued to their screens, watching and listening to his every word.

"We have come to bring harmony to your world and lead my children into their destiny. The Peace for which you have strived, but failed to attain, will be a reality. The lion shall lay down with the lamb, the poor will inherit all worldly things and become rich, the bad will become good and we shall all rejoice. We will show you things that have been hidden from the beginning, but now can be shared. You will understand the relationships and the bonds that we all share. We will introduce you to indescribable pleasures that are yours for the asking. Intimacy and closeness, true love, fulfillment of your desires; these will be my gift to you." The warmth of his message flooded the minds of most of his listeners, but a few resisted.

This stunning visitor told his audience that he was bringing magnificent examples of new technology with him and he intended to share them with the world. Most importantly he emphasized; his mission on earth was to bring peace to mankind. Then the alien commander issued his invitation, first naming every major country on earth, then he continued, "The time has come for the transition into the eternity and the leaders of all the countries I have mentioned must come together and learn the truth. I will host a meeting in two days with a representative from each of these countries, I will be contacting every nation's leader and make the arrangements; each representative will be picked up and transported to the conference room here. Your representatives will be treated with the utmost kindness and respect, assure them they are my honored guests and I personally guarantee their safety. We will be discussing and explaining some of the marvelous secrets of the universe." The alien commander paused for a moment before continuing.

"I understand how perplexing all this may seem, especially to those of you who hold strong beliefs that seem to be in contradiction with what I'm saying. Spending all your earthly life believing certain things are true can make it very difficult to accept new information that seems to be contradictory. Let me assure the religious leaders of the world and their congregations, that our existence and appearance at this time is not a contradiction but a fulfillment of what you believe. I will be holding a meeting for all 'Acknowledged' religious leaders of the world five days from now. Your national leaders having already returned from their meeting will be able to assure you of the importance of the information I will share with you. Once you are 'Acknowledged', you'll be told where to go to be transported to the location of your meeting. I encourage all religious leaders, no matter the size of your congregation, to become 'Acknowledged' so you can righteously represent your flock. My representatives will be available immediately after this broadcast to help you get registered and then acknowledged by me as a known religious leader. We will be superimposing contact information on all of your commercial broadcasts for the next few days, so every one of my children knows how to contact one of my representatives.

"I know how difficult this will be for some of our religious leaders but believe me you need to hear the truth. You need to sit down and listen to what I have to say, then you will know what to tell your people." Looking into the camera with his dark piercing eyes he said, "It has been a very long time since I have been with you, misconceptions have developed over thousands of years, and it is time to set the record of history straight. It is important for you to hear the truth and take the next step in the evolution of mankind." The glorious alien commander continued to look straight into the camera as he spoke.

"Do not fear us my children, we come in peace. Our goal is to bring you the tools mankind needs to lead a peaceful and prosperous life forever." The camera zoomed in on the extraterrestrial leader, and focused on those eyes, as he continued, "Yes my children forever, for I bring you the greatest gift of all; life without death."

A tall thin man stood motionlessly in front of a TV monitor in his office. On his left hand was a wedding ring he had worn for over twenty years, and on his desk sat a picture of his wife with their two teenage daughters and ten-year-old son. On the wall hung a plain wooden cross and on an old tea cart in the corner of the office was a manger scene left from last Christmas. As the man sat down at his desk still watching the TV screen and listening to the voice, the door opened, and someone entered his office.

"Hey, Joe! Have you seen what's on TV! Oh...Um...You have it on."

"Shhhhhhhhh," Joe hissed. "I'm trying to listen."

A cold shiver was already overtaking him. The feeling started the moment Joe heard the alien's voice, and fear began to creep into his inter-being as he listened to the words the alien was speaking. It didn't sound amazing and intriguing to him; it sounded evil and was distressing. When the broadcast ended Joe turned to his friend and said, "I don't know Harry I have a bad feeling about this."

Joe's cell phone began to play a tune that announced his wife's calls. He pressed the receive button and said, "Hi, honey, how are you? No, let me guess. You've been watching TV again?"

"Hey, I'll talk to you later," his friend said and left the room.

"Oh my gawd, Joe, what's happening? Who are those people? Joey, I'm so afraid." It was his wife Judith; he could tell she was a wreck. She hadn't called him Joey in ten years. Judith was emotional to say the least. She lost both of her parents early in her twenties and bore her scars publicly. The delivery of their son was very difficult, and she had been convinced she was going to die during delivery. Their lives seemed to change at that point; they drifted away and became distant from each other. Judith's path led her into education and the past three years she'd been teaching at the local community college. Judith had always been nonpolitical, but when she went back to college all of that changed. Her political views moved steadily to the left, she got involved in the feminist movement as well as marched for every other radical organization in the area. It was tough on Joe to watch his wife slip away, but he had no idea how to stop the slide. The biggest blow came when she participated, with all three children, in a woman's march supporting abortion.

Judith belonged to a nondenominational Christian church that was only ten blocks from their house, but Joe hadn't been to church regularly in many years. He went to church for weddings and funerals, but that was about it. He studied the Bible and sought out teachers on his own and learned how to check out what they taught. He wasn't a born-again Christian, oddly enough, he'd been raised Roman Catholic. Joe had gone to either Catholic school or catechism all the way through high school. There was just too much of it he didn't buy, the first crack for him appeared when suddenly one day at school, around the age of thirteen, they told him he could eat meat on Friday. Before that moment, he knew in his heart; if he ever ate meat on Friday his soul would die and burn in hell. Then suddenly, out of nowhere and without warning, it was okay to go to McDonald's and have a cheeseburger on Friday! *Something is wrong here*, he remembered thinking. *How can it be!? It is a mortal sin*, he thought. *Something smells in Denmark*.

From there, it went downhill, confession to a priest, Joe could not find it in the Bible. The infallibility of the Pope, not there. And he knew several brothers and priests from school, that were obviously gay, Joe always thought that was hypocritical. Then the child molestation stories began to emerge, and he became convinced that the "celibacy of the priesthood" was a crock.

"Joe, he said life without death! Can you believe it? This is what you have always talked about, life everlasting, for the eternity! Joe, they are going to help us, give us amazing things, life everlasting!"

"Listen, Judith, this is not right, this is not good. There's something wrong here believe me I can feel it," Joe replied.

"No, you listen to me, Joe. This is proof now, I told you the Rapture was true. Oh, you would never believe me, but I told you. He's going to fly us away to eternity!"

The rapture, Joe thought, *Hunt the souls to make them fly… (Ezekiel 13:20). Judith wouldn't know that verse,* Joe shook his head. He didn't say anything, he knew where the conversation would go. It always amazed him, not just Judith but with most of the Christians he knew; how so many thought they were going to fly away before Antichrist arrived.

Studying the Bible, Joe had learned many things; many of the mysteries of life had been explained. He knew about the Age that existed before this one, the one where Satan tried to overthrow God. He knew why we were put here on earth; to give all those souls that did not stand with God a chance to choose between good and evil, while they are in the flesh.

"Slow down, you have to think this thing out Judith," Joe said. "We have to go to Scripture. You think this is Jesus returned? Judith, I've tried to tell you before, the false Christ comes first."

"Stop it!" Judith screamed into the phone. "It's so obvious, but not to you! The self-righteous Joe Domingo thinks he knows so much about the Bible. You wouldn't know the truth if it jumped up and bit you!" Judith slammed her cell phone on the table so hard it disconnected the call. Joe shook his head and smiled at the irony of it all. *Judith knows nothing of God's word, except what that dawdling old preacher at her church tells her,* Joe thought. *The only thing that guy teaches is baptism and rapture, he probably thinks the sermon on the mount was a speech Jesus delivered sitting on a horse!*

Joe's frustration was simmering; he thought he might as well bring it to the boiling point. He punched in the number. His brother George had rebelled against all religion at an early age. Although he was now a strict secular, Joe didn't think he had dismissed God totally, but George hadn't acknowledged the existence of God since he was a small child. Joe needed to get his brother's take on these earthshaking events.

As Joe listened to the cell phone for his brother's voice, he thought back on the last time he tried to talk to his brother about God and religion. It hadn't gone well.

"Hello, Joe," George answered the call. "Let me guess you called to apologize."

"Apologize?" Joe questioned. "What are you talking about?"

"Simple, bro, I know you're calling about the aliens. I've always told you there was life out there in the universe and they would be coming to visit us, now it's obvious I was right. I figured you must be calling me to apologize for all that stupid Christian crap you have been spewing for years." The silence seemed to last for a year although it was only a few seconds.

"Well," Joe began, "I guess you already answered my question. You're buying into the whole thing?"

"What is the matter with you Joe? You're looking at it happen right before your eyes and you still can't admit I was right. I've told you for years there was intelligent life out there, now you come face-to-face with it and you're still in denial. What is it going to take to wake you up? They're here, Joe. They are here! They're bringing us knowledge, new exciting technology that we can use right now, Joe."

George went on and on about how many solar systems, and how many planets there were, and how Joe had been idiotic to think that we're the only life forms in the universe. "This is the biggest thing that's ever happened in our lifetime! Face it dude! You're on the wrong side of the fence on this one!"

"Okay, George, hold on a minute. How is it over there on the other side of the fence? You know what I've told you all along. We're going to be challenged when the Antichrist returns. He's going to have a story everybody's going to believe. George, there's something seriously wrong here. The fake Messiah is going to deceive everyone except God's elect. George, are you there?" There was no answer, but Joe was not surprised, his brother wasn't much of a conversationalist when the topic didn't suit him.

"I feel like something terrible is going on George, when I watched him on TV I felt something inside me that was very strange and very dark." Joe spoke the words into the phone knowing there was no one on the other end; he needed to say the words. He slumped into his desk chair and took a deep breath. *What the hell is going on?* he wondered.

Marilyn Nova had been off air for less than a minute, and the enormity of the announcement she just covered overwhelmed her. Marilyn was a field reporter for ADC News, stationed in Israel, and she just witnessed the most amazing event of her entire life. She was assigned to cover exclusively, the good-looking extraterrestrial who seemed to be running the show, and now she had just broken the news story of her life. The name of this handsome stranger from another planet, who seemed to be able to be in more than one place at the same time, was announced to the world by her.

"Sardinian (Sar-din-e-an) is how you pronounce his name," she had announced on air. "He assures me that his mission here on earth is peaceful." Marilyn had been raised Southern Baptist but had rebelled against the strictness of their doctrine at an early age. She had found a Christian Bible teacher years later that opened her eyes to the truth of God's word and she had studied it fervently for years. What she had just witnessed had drained her physically, but it hadn't shaken her faith, she was confident God would lead her to the answers she needed. She needed to know exactly what this meant to her beliefs, she knew God could create life anywhere He wanted, anywhere in the universe. But that didn't seem to be what Sardinian was inferring.

It was more like he was saying…he was responsible for us…somehow. He wasn't specific, and those eyes…I couldn't stop looking into those eyes. I know what he was saying, what he meant. He was inferring he is our father and we are his children, Marilyn's mind was racing.

Washington, DC

Bishop Hayden entered the compartment and knelt before the confessional screen. The Bishop knew it wouldn't be long before it would be his turn to sit on the other side and listen to others' sins and questions. He would need some answers. When the confessional screen slid open, the Bishop said, "Bless me father for I have sinned it has been two weeks since my last confession…"

The confession turned out to be more of a discussion, Father Ramirez had questions of his own. The two men discussed the events of the day and decided they should pray for an answer. Father Ramirez gave the Bishop absolution and closed the sliding panel of the confessional booth. Both men felt lost and had no real convection about what was going on. What did this mean to the Church? To Christianity in general? What would this do to their Christian faith? So many questions and no answers, the two men felt more confused than ever before. Confusion was running rampant.

May 2

It was 10:00 a.m. Pacific Coast Time, Sardinian was again on every TV screen across the globe at the same time. His announcement was shocking; he was providing the world with a new power source. He explained that this was a power source that had been used on earth before; the last time he visited. Sardinian said he had taken the equipment with him when he left, mankind at the time, he said, had not been ready for such technology. Sardinian told the world; at that very moment, his people were fitting many of the monoliths across the globe with apparatus that would form a power grid to transmit energy throughout the world. No more power bills, electricity will live in the air, just turn your air conditioner on and it will run!

"This will bring more equality to the world," Sardinian said. "A new day is dawning on earth…."

On CNN News, one of their most professional news anchors was interviewing one of Sardinian's lieutenants, the alien was a handsome young man with flowing black hair. The anchor, a young, well-endowed redheaded from Philly, was obviously enamored with the extraterrestrial. You could almost see the electricity sparking between them during the segment. When the interview was over the extraterrestrial took the woman by the hand and led her down the hall toward the front door.

May 4

The invasion was quick and unopposed; Sardinian's lieutenants overwhelmed the world. Thousands upon thousands of the beautiful male-looking visitors inhabited cities and towns, large and small, setting up their headquarters and establishing the new law. Sardinian's Law it would come to be called and it tweaked things on earth more than a little. Humans were told to prepare for the eternity, and to do that mankind would need to take on some "eternal behaviors" that was still alien to earthlings. Traditional marriage was out the window. "As Jesus taught," Sardinian announced, "we do not marry in the eternity, read Mark 12:25."

Using scripture to defend and support the aliens' decrees concerning sexual activities became normal procedure in the daily media, and many established denominations embraced the New Religion immediately. It almost seemed as if some had secretly been waiting for Sardinian, ready to do his bidding. Hordes of "Christians" from all denominations as well as all other beliefs worldwide rushed to support the alien and his new doctrine. His lieutenants, like a swarm of ravenous locust, descended upon the masses converting and baptizing them in the name of Sardinian. By the end of May, even the Muslim leaders began to fold. Motivated by unlimited wealth, they joined Sardinian and his New Religion, eager to participate in the unbridled wealth and power they saw possible. They were eager to rule the masses through the eternity alongside their new god.

"Jesus, as you know him, is one of my most powerful defenders," Sardinian taught the Christians. "He will be returning soon and stand by my right-side, but now you all must prepare yourselves for the journey into the eternity. You must ready yourselves for your eternal destiny."

Sardinian made another announcement even more amazing than the revelation that traditional marriage would be abandoned; his proclamation was met with shock and awe.

"From this time forward, as we prepare to enter the eternity," Sardinian announced with authority. "I am closing the woman's womb. From this moment on, pregnancies and human births are ended."

A pregnant woman had been a rarity for some time on earth, and the reduction of births worldwide had not gone unnoticed long before Sardinian's appearance. Pollution, global warming, abortion, the increasing use of birth control, dropping male sperm count, and evolving attitudes on childrearing within the youth of the world, had been universally accepted as the causes for the dropping number of pregnancies and births. Many leaders worldwide had acclaimed the dropping birth rate as a step forward in getting the population explosion under control. During the past year, fewer and fewer women had become pregnant, and delivery wards worldwide had been nearly abandoned except for a few exceptions. To no avail, evangelical Christians in America and elsewhere had frantically encouraged their congregations to change this alarming development. Now, if the extraterrestrial made good on his newest announcement the issue would be mute.

Intense meetings took place for several weeks, first with world government and religious leaders, then with those that really run the world, the wealthy. Sardinian and his lieutenants met with the industrial and financial leaders of the world and they made a deal. To the world leaders in government, Sardinian promised continued power and wealth, and to the world's religious leaders, Sardinian promised continued power and wealth. It was simple, acknowledge him and accept his doctrine and the world would be theirs. The leaders would be his kings and governors and the religious leaders would be the priests of his New Religion. It would be the religion of truth that would finally acknowledge the origin of creation and rightfully acknowledge Sardinian as being responsible for human existence and future eternal life. Sardinian offered several examples as proof of his doctrine, and the fact that all people everywhere now had electric appliances that worked without being plugged in to a power source was living proof he spoke the truth. Sardinian explained that most cultures and religions of this world accepted the existence of one Almighty God, and they all strove for peace and preached the eternity. "Over thousands of years," Sardinian taught, "the universal truth has been mixed up and mis-reported by man."

In the beginning, the meetings held with the economic and financial powers of the world went much faster than those with the clergy; their talk was all about money, most cared very little about the doctrine Sardinian was preaching. However, the wealthy's disinterest in Sardinian's Doctrine was short-lived; they became very attentive as soon as he began speaking about everlasting life. Once the eternity and the things that were possible through his amazing powers were on the table, they were all ears. Suddenly he became very important to the wealthy of the world; when they saw the possibility of being powerful and wealthy forever. Many well-known entrepreneurs of the world were anxious to become part of his movement and be visible to the masses. They were familiar with unbridled power and wanted to maintain their status into the eternity, Sardinian was offering them that opportunity.

"I come from a planet in the Pleiades, in the constellation Taurus," Sardinian revealed. "Things are different there, the atmosphere bolsters the flesh rather than deteriorates it. It regenerates and energizes the flesh. You will see when you get there, it is our eternal home, what you call heaven."

The scientific community of the world marveled out loud at the advanced understanding Sardinian was sharing with the world. Almost immediately the world of science declared their support for and belief in the scientific truth that in certain atmospheric conditions the flesh body could live forever without aging. Revivals followed, then more meetings, and they were magnificent. The world was invited to the REVIVAL OF ALL TIME, and Sardinian and his lieutenants were in charge. The first converts to his new religion, were the leaders of the world; bankers, kings, religious leaders, and they all embraced Sardinian's Doctrine. A new baptism was required to wash away the sins and misconceptions of this earthly flesh age. Sardinian took over most of the temples, churches and other places of worship of the world and set up shop with his own religion, and the masses followed their leaders.

Along with free power the people of the world were given free clean water wherever they lived. Sardinian's lieutenants handed out an amazing contraption that, when placed in water of any kind, would sucked it in and pumped out clean pure delicious water, twenty-four hours a day, seven days a week. Sardinian also promised that he would soon provide the people of earth with a new technological marvel that would change all the world's desert wastelands into lush green forests and jungles.

After Sardinian had given the world these new scientific advancements, most believed that every word out of Sardinian's mouth was gospel. The people of the world, regardless of their former nationality, religious affiliation, or economic status rushed to Sardinian's revivals, were baptized and entered "training" for the eternity. Mothers and daughters, fathers and sons alike flocked to the revivals, and after baptism, their training began preparing them for the coming eternity. Many of the things they were taught were amazing and some seemed to explain mysteries they had wondered about all their lives. It was evident that their days of having decaying flesh bodies were numbered, and the Doctrine told them they needed to prepare for the journey to their new home. Sardinian promised not only an end to aging but a reversal in the flesh that would return them to their youth forever. The evidence was undeniable, how could there be any doubt? Sardinian and his lieutenants were so powerful, so knowledgeable, and were bringing mankind prosperity and peace, how could anyone question them? But a few did.

The Doctrine was clear and simple; in many ways it mirrored the Ten Commandments, but there were differences. Of course, Sardinian was to be acknowledged as supreme father and God. It was obvious that these visitors were more powerful than any human on earth and they were going to help the people live forever. Sardinian appointed the most well-known and respected religious leaders of the world to be his liaisons to the people, it was hard to argue against. But a few did.

May 17

Marilyn Nova was working on a spot for that evening's news broadcast, and the subject matter for her report was a familiar one. She had reported several times on the two old men who had been preaching to the Jews and the Christians in the streets of Jerusalem. What had attracted the most attention was their ability to seemingly heal people of very serious conditions. They were very similar in their teaching but didn't seem to be connected in any other way. They arrived unannounced in Jerusalem a few days before the alien spacecrafts began to watch over the major cities of the world. Marilyn didn't know their real names, they went by nicknames; the Christian preacher was called The Lawyer and the Jew was called Zeke. The lawyer's nickname seemed reasonable since the main subject of his preaching was how the Law, or in other words the Ten Commandments, were impossible to live by and how Jesus Christ's death on the cross relieved us of the burden of the Law through His forgiveness of our sins. Zeke's nickname didn't seem to fit as snuggly, his singular message was one of repentance for your sins. Everyone was focused on their mysterious ability to heal people.

Marilyn's story tonight would describe the meeting of the two men today at the Temple in Jerusalem. They seemed to be totally independent of each other at first, but that suddenly began to change. The crowd was large, and many seemed to be cured of various ailments by the two men. Marilyn personally knew one of the people healed, he was a crew person who worked for her camera man. He had been born with a club foot; it made him walk with a limp. The Lawyer seemed to cure his ailment when he placed his hands upon the crewman's head and prayed. Marilyn felt a presence engulf the crowd at the time of the healing, it was amazing! She knew it was for real, the boy that was cured was overcome with joy and praised the Lord Jesus Christ loudly.

Zeke was performing similar miracles on the Jewish side of the crowd. As time went by, the two men were engulfed by the crowd and mystically seemed to flow toward each other. Slowly the crowd churned as if it was a living organism gently nudging the two men toward each other. When they finally met and looked into each other's eyes it was as if they recognized a long-lost friend, then they suddenly embraced each other. Then as the press successfully surrounded the two old men, firing questions at both, they seemed to turn their back on the reporters and disappeared into...the crowd. But that didn't seem possible to Marilyn, they had been surrounded by reporters.

Marilyn Nova knew the prophecies concerning the Two Witnesses, and her mind was racing. Sifting through everything she had ever learned about the End Times, the Antichrist, and the Two Witnesses. She had felt the Spirit, she knew in her heart that the time had come.

CHAPTER 19

The Summer

June 3
Washington, DC

The office was dark when he returned to it, it was late, and he sighed deeply as he reached out and turned on the light. It had been a very long day and all Joe could think about was getting some sleep. He'd been sleeping on this couch for the past two weeks, and after the scene that took place tonight at his home, he thought he would probably be taking up permanent residency here. Frustration mixed with anger had gotten the best of him and he lost his temper. He always tried to be the calm one, the one that kept his wits about himself. Judith was screaming that he was an infidel, she had just told him she was sending their two teenage daughters to go through training in the Doctrine. They had been "specially picked" she proudly told him, the beautiful young alien they called Dreyfus said their daughters were "above average." He said the boy would be ready for training next month.

Joe was desperate, "You can't do that, Judith, I won't let you."

"You can't stop me! What are you gonna tell the judge? Are you gonna tell him you don't believe in the Doctrine? They will lock you up! They'll put you down in a hole where you belong! They're looking for you now, Joe. I told them all about you today. Where have you been staying anyway? Probably on skid row somewhere." Luckily, Joe had never told Judith anything about his "office"; it was his man-cave where he sometimes sold advertising for a local radio station and sometimes worked on a book he was writing. He needed his hideout now more than ever, it was his haven, but since he knew Judith had reported him, he knew he would have to be more careful returning to it tonight.

Joe blew his top. "You are going to send our daughters away with those beasts? Do you have any idea what you're doing?" Joe screamed. That was when it hit him; the anger and frustration was because he knew there was nothing, he could do about it. So he left.

Joe had a pretty good idea what interested these so-called aliens—from the accounts in the Book of Genesis. He was frantic, he had to stop this, but he had no idea what to do. So he prayed.

June 5
Israel

Sardinian filled every TV screen across the globe, again. This time his speech was more about organization and training rather than the Doctrine. He laid out how their transitioning trip to the eternity was going to take place, step by step. He introduced the idea of an Academy that all converts to his New Religion would be required to attend. The Academy would be the official school for training converts, and graduation from the first phase of the Academy would earn the graduate merit points which would translate into credits that could be used to buy material things until they traveled to their new home.

After each new phase of the Academy, the graduate would again be reevaluated and rewarded for their hard work. All new converts needed to do was pledge their allegiance to their new god, Sardinian. The locations across the continents were announced where the people could enroll in the Academy and begin their training toward the eternity. Sardinian stressed that all should come and enjoy the Great Revival. Sardinian inferred that time was short and that delay might cost the converts their eternal life.

Marilyn Nova was wrapping up her television report for ADC News in Jerusalem on the latest announcements to the world by the alien Sardinian. She had been working for several weeks on a story that interested her very much. The story's question was; what was happening with all the young people that had been taken to alien ships across the world? Very few had emerged from the ships and a small group of parents who had supported their children's indoctrination into Sardinian's new religion were beginning to have questions. Some mothers had been invited to join their children on the ships and experience the journey to eternity with them, but none of those women had returned either. Marilyn was sure there was something heinous going on behind the scenes that would change everyone's perception of these uninvited visitors, she thought she knew what was happening, but the rest of the world was blind to the truth.

Marilyn was speaking the final sentence of her latest report when she saw out of the corner of her eye someone she recognized. The woman was standing next to one of Sardinian's lieutenants, and Marilyn was sure she recognized her from a few weeks back. She had been covering a story about several Jewish moms trying to visit their daughters in training. She had spoken to the woman for several minutes about her daughter and how excited she was about joining her daughter in this unknown adventure, just before she boarded an alien craft. What convinced Marilyn this was the same woman was her unique beauty and good looks. Now looking at her from a distance, she was still strikingly beautiful, but she had changed. Marilyn could see it in her face, a lost distant look that could not be disguised. No longer was the confident air visible which the woman had displayed previously, her demeanor spoke of subservience and the alien she was with obviously controlled her.

Marilyn worked her way through the crowd getting closer to the woman. When the reporter got close enough to ask a question, she spoke in soft, quiet voice hoping not to gain the alien's attention. "How's your daughter," Marilyn cautiously asked the woman. As the woman's attention turned toward Marilyn, so did that of the alien.

"There you are," the alien drawled before the woman could speak. "I was wondering what happened to you, I've been thinking a lot about the beautiful reporter from ADC. I have been looking forward to getting to know you better." The magnificent-looking creature with long, flowing hair reached to take Marilyn by the hand, but she turned and ran in the opposite direction. Marilyn ran as fast as she could, pushing her way through the crowd of people. She didn't stop running for several minutes, and when she did, she was completely out of breath. Marilyn stood bent over heaving, gasping for air, but one thing was indelibly burned into her memory. It was the smell. It was the smell that had come from the glorious creature. It was a semi-sweet pleasant smell, subtle and inviting, and to Marilyn's dismay it had been very sexually stimulating. Marilyn was shaking uncontrollably, the alien's words ricocheted around her mind: "I have been looking forward to getting to know you better."

Anticipation was high; it had been building for weeks. Sardinian had announced that he would publish in writing all the information about his "Academy" and the merit point system that was involved. From what Sardinian had said before, converts believed that his merit-based point system would lead to financial rewards that would follow them into the eternity, they were hoping for confirmation. The date for this publication had been set, June 5 would be the day, and now the moment had arrived. Sardinian had promised that the full details about the path to eternity would be published worldwide today!

Newspapers everywhere sold out within minutes of hitting the street. Everyone wanted a copy of the path of their destiny. There it was in black and white in every newspaper across the world. The Academy, the areas of the Doctrine that must be studied, and the grading system that would allow people to pass to the next level. Sardinian's decree specified the points to be awarded at the completion of each level, and the merit system for other activities by which converts could earn points outside the Academy. It was all cut and dried, so simple. First pledge allegiance unto death to Sardinian and his New Religion of "truth," then work and worship and earn. The world rejoiced at the news; go to the Academy, learn the truth, then live life eternal in luxury. The world rejoiced. But a few did not.

June 30

Joe didn't leave his office for days after his last meeting with Judith, he didn't feel safe out in the open any longer. Then, he had begun wearing disguises when he went out in public, and eventually, Joe got pretty good at becoming someone else. He led his own information reconnaissance mission concerning his family, and what he discovered crushed him. His entire family had boarded metallic discs; first his daughters, then a week later, Judith and his son. No one had seen or heard from them again and two of Sardinian's lieutenants had moved into his house and declared themselves judges in his old community. They announced that any disputes or problems concerning the New Religion were to be handled through them.

The President of the United States had not announced his support for Sardinian yet and had been holding a hardline against the aliens, saying he was looking into things. The president ordered that all legal disputes were to be temporarily left to judges and public officials already in place who had pledged allegiance to the United States of America not Sardinian. For the time being, this left aliens very little to do in America and tensions were becoming strained, yet Sardinian didn't move against the president.

Joe hung out at different shopping malls across the city and became a regular at the food court's that populated them. He would sit by himself and listen. Very seldom would Joe engage in conversation with others, but whenever he did, no matter what the subject, he made sure they thought he agreed with everything they said. His response was always "Ummm" or "Ahhhhh," while nodding his head affirmatively.

"Isn't it great what's happening in the world? The eternity is coming brother, isn't it wonderful?"

"Ahhhhh," Joe would respond.

"Did you hear his Holiness's latest speech? Oh, he's so awesome, isn't he?"

"Ummm," Joe would answer.

Joe noticed some oddities amongst the people that came up to him to talk; he never approached anyone on his own. They were always male, of course there weren't many women around anymore, especially young pretty ones. There were some older women, but they always seemed to be in some type of trance. It was eerie; Joe saw them everywhere he went, women wandering around with a glaze over their eyes. They were almost zombie like, going here going there, hardly ever speaking to anyone. Joe knew by now these women must have been called to a meeting on a metallic discs but had been sent back to work here on earth. These women were not spying, they didn't seem to pay much attention to anything, they were too busy. They were working on projects for the aliens, printing posters, writing scripts, running errands of all kinds.

The men are the spies, Joe thought.

The men that took time to approach and talk to him were all very inquisitive. They all asked one specific question: "Have you been to the Academy?" This was the only time Joe would ever deviate from his standard "Ummm" or "Ahhhhh," he would simply say "I'm going next week! Can't wait!" It seemed to satisfy them, they were obviously looking for dissenters, and Joe never gave them a clue of his real thoughts.

Now Joe was searching frantically for some news on a report he had received from the Christian Underground. The rumor was that the two "would be prophets," the two old men who seemed older than time, had publicly denounced Sardinian as a fake on Israeli TV. His source told him the two men had been interviewed by an ADC reporter in Jerusalem the day before, and somehow the video report made it "on air" one time before it was squashed. Around noon another source gave him an email address and told him to contact the person for a link to the interview. The pressure to shut down adverse news was intense, and the source told Joe that he must be very careful with whom he shared this information. There was no one Joe trusted enough anymore to share his lunch with let alone this link. He sent an email and received a response almost immediately. There wasn't a link to a website, the video itself was attached.

The video was a little grainy, but Joe could easily make out the two old men with beards and long hair. They were dressed in tattered clothing; Joe thought the cloths looked like they would have been thrown away by the Goodwill. The audio was excellent, and Joe understood every word. The interviewer was a woman, very nice-looking, which was odd to see these days. He didn't catch her name, *Marilyn something*, he thought. She asked the prophets several questions about who they were and where they came from, but their answers were very vague. They said things like "We are messengers," and "we are the conscience of mankind." They said they came from far away and were blessed by the grace of God, but they had not been vague about Sardinian.

"He is evil. He is a liar, don't believe what he says," they warned. "He is not what he seems to be." The woman reporter seemed agitated searching hard for her next words.

"Is…is he Satan?" the woman asked the two prophets in what came out as almost a whisper.

"He is Death," the man they called Zeke shouted. Joe fell to his knees and praise the Lord.

Powerful world and global leaders had been pushing for world peace since the 1960s, but as nuclear abilities accelerated, out of fear, opposing views became closer. As world powers, with the help of the UN, forged a makeshift alliance between previous foes in the East and West; hopes for peace also accelerated. Russia and the United States had been opposed to each other for decades, and although an important economic partner, China had become more and more aggressive toward the United States and Israel militarily. The World Peace Conference, which had given mankind so much promise, had fallen apart when the United States and Israel withdrew from the talks, just before the metallic discs from another world appeared. The United States and Israel had refused to bend to what they believe were immoral positions taken by the group involving human rights. Iran and Syria, along with the kings of the East and most Arab nations were intent on their centuries old agendas. Some Muslim nations insisted that Sharia law be recognized as the accepted method of mediation. The United States and Israel could not accept their demands and therefore pulled out of the coalition.

Shortly after that, the discs appeared and the hopes for world peace were revived because of Sardinian's promises. In two short months, things had changed drastically, because by the middle of July, the world powers were at each other's throats again. Israel was surrounded by its enemies and was the target of hostile demands. The Palestinians, who were supported by Iran, were pressuring Israel to relinquish Jerusalem, claiming it was their rightful homeland. China was threatening the United States over Taiwan and the China Sea, and Russia was taking the side of anyone who was against Israel and the United States. Except for the support of the United States, Israel stood alone surrounded by its enemies in the Middle East.

Sardinian's gifts to the world had helped the common man tremendously, but it also helped the powerful governments of the world in their quests for power. Unlimited electric power, clean water, and billions of dollars of Sardinian economic credits created a windfall for their hidden nuclear programs. Sardinian had forbidden nations to continue with their research, but just as the world powers had cheated in the past; they lied to Sardinian and they continued with their secret development programs. The proclamations, of the pre-viously obscure "Holy Men of Israel," had leaked to the world and their videos had gone viral on social media. Videos speaking against Sardinian were appearing everywhere, and although they usually vanished as soon as they appeared, the videos kept coming. Sardinian's support from the world leaders was weakening as they began to believe they might have to survive without him. Already possessing many of Sardinian's gifts, they saw no reason to share them with the common people and sought a way to possibly even use them against Sardinian himself, if necessary. After all, the alien had shown no proof he could deliver on his promise of eternal life.

By the middle of July, the United States and Israel had been isolated, and by August 1, Russia and China had joined forces against them. Sardinian had taken control the Temple Mount, his golden throne was placed there, and communion was being taken to him all over the world. Sardinian sent a constant flow of proclamations claiming his authority as god throughout the world, demanding the world powers stand down. World leaders gave his orders lip service and promised to obey but they continued their military deployments against the United States and Israel undaunted. Cracks had appeared in the alliances Sardinian had forged with world powers. His parlor tricks no longer seemed to mesmerize world leaders as they had in the beginning, Sardinian would soon have to demonstrate his supernatural power to the world.

August 2

Getting a flight to Israel wasn't the easiest thing to accomplish these days, but Joe had made some strong connections in the Christian Underground, and now he was only a few minutes away from touchdown in the Holy Land. From the first time he saw the old preachers on television, he knew he had to go and seek them out. Through the Underground, he was able to contact the ADC reporter who had interviewed the Lawyer and Zeke, and after speaking with her, Joe was convinced she knew the truth. He made an appointment to meet her for dinner this evening and was shocked when she accepted his invitation. She knew the hotel he was staying at and agreed to meet him in the lobby at seven. Somehow, he knew that she knew that he knew. The Holy Spirit seemed to be growing in him and he was learning to trust what *It* told him. He understood things he never knew about before, and his discernment of people and groups was razor-sharp and true. During their telephone conversation he could hear the reporter's relief, and knew she realized that she had found one more person who knew the truth.

The oval office was dark, but the president hadn't been napping, he was praying. Being vice president for eight years to the most popular president in modern history had helped him win his hard-fought campaign for the presidency. His opponent on the left had tried to make a point of concern with the public over the vice president's hard-core Christian beliefs. It hadn't worked, and he was swept into office on the coattails of the man he served for eight years. He had a very close relationship with his Lord and Savior and spoke often to Him in prayer. The president believed that God not only watched over him, but often led him. He was sure the moves he had made concerning Sardinian were correct because he had been careful to consult the Lord on all important matters.

His staff knew not to disturb the president at these times although they never quite grasped the actual importance of these sessions. He was worried about Russia and China and the dangerous game they were playing. He knew the Palestinians would never settle for anything less than the extinction of Israel. And he felt sure standing against the human rights violations being committed in Africa, the Middle East, and in the countries formerly belonging to the old Soviet Union was the right thing to do. The President, in his heart, believed refusing to surrender to the incredible inhuman demands being made, including the institution of Sharia Law in many countries, was God's will.

Most of all he believed, he knew through the grace of God, that Sardinian was not who he claimed to be. From the first time the President had heard the strange alien speak he knew this creature had evil intent. He watched and took note of what Sardinian was doing, he tested the fruit. Sardinian had brought more danger and distress to the earth than all his free electricity and clean water were worth. If the genocide of millions of people and the abuse of women and children worldwide was fruit from Sardinian's tree, the president didn't want to eat of it. The president believed he and the prime minister of Israel were doing God's work, for the benefit of mankind. So the president of the United States of America continued to pray in the dark.

Joe was as antsy as a cat on a hot tin roof; perspiration was leaving his body like rats fleeing a sinking ship. He recognized her as soon as she entered the room and made a beeline to her side. Marilyn was everything Joe had expected and more. She was bright and savvy, and she knew exactly what was going on. Sardinian wasn't our father; God of heaven and earth. He was the evil one, the serpent, the devil, the false Christ and was here to deceive the world. Dinner was spent filling each other in on not only their pasts but their present situations, and they shared their theories about what was happening now and why. They discussed the mysteries that were so baffling. They agreed the number of missing women all over the world was alarming, and Marilyn shared with Joe what she thought it was all about. She told him about her encounter with Sardinian's lieutenant, and the odd alluring, sexually stimulating odor that the alien seemed able to project at her. Tears welled up in Joe's eyes; Marilyn reached out and grabbed his hand.

"What's the matter, Joe? Did I say something to offend you?" Joe shook his head and told Marilyn about his wife and children. They sat in silence for a long time; finally Joe took a deep breath and spoke.

"Marilyn, we have to be careful they have been after me in the states, my wife...my ex-wife told them about me and they did their best to track me down." Marilyn nodded as if to say she understood totally. She explained to Joe what she thought Sardinian's lieutenant wanted with her and said she had no doubt he would have his way with her if he could find her now. She had been too afraid to go back to work after that incident. Marilyn had immediately deserted her apartment and had never gone back to work. She threw her cell phone in the Euphrates and bought a burner. Her minister for many years in the states, succeeded in getting her a message giving her his new cell phone number, and when she called him, he explained what had been happening to him. He also had gone underground; most of his congregation had flocked to Sardinian's New Religion. When some of his most fervent parishioners tried to convince him to simply listen to what the aliens had to say, he refused. He had been visiting a sick parishioner when they came to his house looking for him. Luckily, he watched it all from his laptop as the webcams throughout his house revealed their activities. First, they went through his files and took a list of his parishioners along with some other private papers. Then they ransacked his bedroom, living room, and office; it seemed there was something in particular they were after, but he had no idea what it was. He never went back to his house again. Her pastor told Marilyn about the Christian Underground, and she contacted them immediately.

Joe told her he wanted to meet the two prophets, he was sure they were the Two Witnesses of the Bible, and she agreed. The problem was, Marilyn said she had no idea where to find them, they would always find her through her producer when she had interviewed them. Now, Marilyn had no idea where they were or how to contact them, they just seemed to appear in different places at different times unannounced. Marilyn told Joe she believed her producer might still know how to contact the Lawyer and Zeek.

"It might be dangerous," she warned. "I don't know where my producer is with all this, Joe. He may have joined Sardinian's group for all I know. He's Jewish and sort of an introvert and, he was never very religious...I just don't know."

They decided it was worth the risk.

August 4

Marilyn finally heard back from her friend Earl Schmidt, she knew he had an inside track on the Prophets' appearances when she was still working at ADC and she hoped he still did. Earl had been born and raised in Jerusalem and educated in Judaism. He never let anyone know what his religious beliefs were but coming from a devout Jewish family everyone assumed he was too. Actually, Earl had converted to Christianity several years earlier giving his life to Jesus Christ. Earl did not, however, inform his family of his conversion, and studied Scripture quietly on his own. Earl worried how the revelation of his conversion would affect his elderly mother's health; she was eighty-seven and would not easily accept his conversion.

Marilyn was encouraged when she heard Earl's story. He told her he had made his connection with the Prophets and the Christian Underground on the same day.

"Most important day of my life," Earl Schmidt told her. He had fallen in with the Lawyer the first day he appeared and became his secret disciple immediately. The reason Marilyn and the camera crew always got to the site of an appearance just minutes before the Prophets arrived was because they planned it that way. Earl had become the two men's publicity manager and Marilyn's reports had become their megaphone, without her even knowing. That same day, the Lawyer gave him a phone number that would connect him to the

Christian Underground, and Earl also became the two prophets' new cameraman. After talking with Marilyn for a short time Earl told her when and where the next appearance of the Two Witnesses would take place.

The next day, Marilyn and Joe were at the Church of the Holy Sepulcher an hour before Earl said the Two Prophets would appear. The traffic outside the church and up the stairs that led to Calvary seemed to be at a normal level, no one was expecting anything out of the ordinary. Earl had told Marilyn the exact area of the appearance, so they waited patiently. As soon as the two bearded men arrived, or perhaps appeared, a small group began to gather. As word spread throughout the city, the crowd grew larger and larger. The message the two men delivered was one of repentance and salvation. They spoke of the first commandment and how important it was to avoid idolatry; they must not worship a false god. Repeatedly they loudly pronounced, "We don't worship Angels!"

They spoke of terrible times coming for those who would worship Sardinian. Then they began healing the people of all their ailments, they healed the blind, and they healed the lame. Earl was busy filming the event, Joe and Marilyn had hoped he would introduce them. But when Joe finally reached the Lawyer, the prophet reached out his hand and touched him on the forehead. "Hello, Joe, you've come a long way to see me," the Lawyer said. Joe was stunned.

"Yes," Joe stuttered, "you know who I am and where I came from?"

"Of course," the Lawyer said to Joe, "you are of the Elect, we know you all," he said as he looked over at Marilyn with a knowing smile.

August 6

Tempers flared, and old hatreds won out. The world was at the point of blowing itself up again, when Sardinian took control of all communication systems worldwide. He took control of all military and commercial communications at the same time, and the world froze. There was only one thing to see no matter where you looked, and it was the image of Sardinian. His speech was short and sweet, the first thing he drove home was that if he could control the communication systems of the world he could also control the weapon systems of the world. He acknowledged there had been a few problems of late with the Resistance but promised peace would soon reign eternal. The last statement Sardinian made, before going off the air, was a direct threat to the powers of the world.

"You should know from the defense systems you encountered the first day you attacked us there is nothing you can do to hurt us. I will not allow my rebellious children to destroy the world I created for them. I want a worldwide truce, and I want it now! Or…you will pay the price."

At this point, no one was about to call his bluff.

The crackdown on the Resistance began in mid-August and steadily intensified. By the end of August, Sardinian had begun a worldwide detainment policy. As Resisters were identified, usually by members of their family or members of their former religious denomination, they were fitted with a wrist band that was a technological wonder. It seemed to be of an unknown material that could not be penetrated, and not only set off a violent charge to the nervous system when a violation occurred, it also sent an uninterrupted signal to the Sardinian headquarters, sending them an enormous amount of information.

The Resistors were not imprisoned, they were simply ordered not to associate with another identified Resister. When two bracelets came within twenty feet of each other, a force was initiated between the Resisters that rendered them zombie like, unable to communicate with anyone. After separating the required distance from each other the Resistors gradually regained their faculties but were subjected to grogginess for days. At first the outcry against this practice was heard worldwide, but those rebellious people were promptly fitted with their own bracelets. In a single day the public protest was quieted, and the Resistance was driven even further underground. Whenever identified Resistors ventured out in public they were reviled by Sardinian's followers or incapacitated when they came too close to another banded Resister.

Only the United States escaped Sardinian's bracelet imprisonment because of the President's resolve. Only the United States was standing strong against the oppressive rule of Sardinian. Most Americans had converted to the New Religion, but still the President would not bend, basing his stand on the Constitution. He was under tremendous pressure from the other two branches of government, yet he was a rock.

Sardinian said the current situation was only temporary, and he promised the Resisters would have their day in court soon. Sardinian also predicted that the members of the Resistance would soon accept the truth and embrace him as their one and only all-powerful God. They would come to their senses and realize the grandeur of his eternity, and he would graciously welcome them into the fold. The goal of all the Resisters became; remain vigilant, and out of sight. Even small groups of people became increasingly scrutinized and socializing was a sure way to get your own piece of Sardinian jewelry.

Joe and Marilyn, along with Earl Smidt, went way underground. These three unlikely rebels took refuge, along with Zeke and the Lawyer, in the ancient tunnels beneath Jerusalem. In a hiding place provided by the Christian Underground, they found themselves living the life of fugitives. They had a small group of individual supporters who supplied them with the necessities.

In the ongoing videos Marilyn acted as interviewer, Joe took over the camera work and Earl was in charge of communications and made sure the videos got on the internet. The one thing that worked in the Resistance's favor was the insatiable appetite the world had developed for the use of the internet and consumption of world news. Even Sardinian could not stem the demand for it. So the channel between the Prophets and the world remained open.

CHAPTER 20

The Fall

September 20

Preparations for Rosh Hashanah, the Feast of Trumpets, were intensifying with the Holy Day only forty-eight hours away. Plans for the televised trials of the Resisters were moving forward at a neck break speed. It had first been announced that no cameras would be allowed at the trials, but the outcry by the public was enormous. Sardinian, feeling the pressure of eroding support in some quarters, reversed the decision banning cameras, and the television world was preparing for the show of a lifetime. The unspoken anticipation of the world media was one of glee, the Sardinian world was preparing for the condemnation of the damnable Resisters, and the hope of the media was they would be televising the actual administration of damnation upon the Resisters. The vision of combusting flames surrounding the infidels was tantalizing the world media; it was going to be the Salem Witch Trials all over again! But this time, they would be there televising them.

Several thousand Resisters had been rounded up, finding them was easy, their bracelets told Sardinian's lieutenants exactly where they were. The trials were to take place in Jerusalem and transporting the discontents was a major undertaking. Thousands of people worldwide were loaded into the metallic disks and flown into the

Holy Land, a camp was set up at Bethlehem in an old abandoned refugee camp. When the Resisters were picked up, the setting of their wrist bands were adjusted. Now, if the Resisters got separated more than twenty feet from another Resister, the zombie-like condition would be imposed upon the person. The Resisters were crammed into the deserted camp, no walls were needed, the thousands of people huddled together day and night and were watched over by armed guards too.

The trials were to start in forty-eight hours, and the hunt for the two old prophets and their aids had also intensified. The group was in hiding somewhere, but as yet had been undiscovered by Sardinian and his army of supporters. Every day, it seemed, a new video would find its way to the internet and then it would find its way into the mainstream media and the nightly news. The Prophets continued hammering Sardinian as a liar and a fake, and some, especially world leaders, were beginning to ask questions. The videos no longer showed large crowds surrounding the Prophets, they were now shot in private secluded places, so the cloud of locust could not find and descend upon them. There had been a couple of close calls, however, and the Prophets and their crew initiated strict new procedures for their own protection.

The room they were in was dimly illuminated by light that filtered down through the tunnels somehow. Their eyes had already adjusted. Their hiding place was located deep in the tunnels that ran beneath the city of Jerusalem, and its entrance was masterfully disguised leaving the appearance of just one of a thousand dead ends in the enormous tunnel system beneath the city. The hideout consisted of seven small rooms connected by a circular tunnel, a ventilation shaft headed up to some unknown location, and it had a bathroom complete with a modern sink and toilet with running water. The underground temperature never seemed to change, never too hot, never too cold. The five fugitives felt like the most hunted people in history, but they also believed that with God's protection, and the help of the Christian Underground they could hold up here for quite a while.

There was one room in their hideout that rendered more light than the others, because of a single hanging bulb powered by some hidden 12-volt source. The bulb burned twenty-four seven, and the room was used mostly for the limited reading and writing that was required for their next appearance. The filming of the Two Prophets needed to be done outside in natural light and getting to different locations for each taping was the most dangerous part of their mission. For security reasons, it was necessary to use a different site for each taping and getting there was problematic. Disguising the three aids was fairly easy but changing the appearance of the two old bearded men was a little more difficult.

Marilyn had come up with a fantastic idea, and the group immediately put it into action. Contacting anyone on the outside seemed dangerous, not only for the five fugitives but also for the loyal friends that would be helping them. This time, the task was so important, the danger was justified. They were asking for specific clothing, disguises for the five fugitives. A nun's habit for Marilyn, two hooded monk robes for Joe and Earl, two extra-large burkas complete with full vials for the two ancient Prophets, and a collection of various other hair and facial accessories. Each of their robes had the official Sardinian "Conversion" insignia embroidered on its right sleeve. The group could move around the city unnoticed and unchallenged. But first, picking the location for the next taping was a top daily priority for the group, and today was no exception.

Marilyn and Earl were the most knowledgeable about possible taping locations in the city, so the final decision was usually left up to them, now the group wanted to do something more spectacular and tomorrow they would attempt a daring mission. The trials were to begin the next day, and to allow the maximum number of people to attend, the International Convention Center Jerusalem had been chosen as the location. The ICC Jerusalem was the largest venue in all of Israel, and Earl knew the perfect place within the property to do their taping.

"There is a private conference room in the east end of the building with its own private bathroom attached, for which I happen to know the door key code." This revelation got everyone's attention.

"There is also a slide bolt on the inside of the door, so we can lock it from the inside. There is also an escape route through an outside window if we need to get away fast, and hopefully with all the construction commotion going on the room will be vacant." Earl continued proudly with a smile, "And the best part is, across the front wall of the room, behind the chairs where we will tape the interview, in glittering silver lettering it reads ICC Jerusalem. Our viewers will know we have entered the serpent's den."

September 21

The trials were to begin the next day, and the International Convention Center was alive with activity, the fugitives wandered around the building unnoticed. The huge influx of visitors from all over the world helped the fugitives elude their hunters, there were so many new people in the Holy City from all over the world there was little chance anyone would take much notice of them. The main stage in the ICC's largest hall, called the Menachem Ussishkin auditorium, was where Sardinian and his crew would sit during the trials; it had seating for over three thousand people. The work crews were still busy bringing in folding chairs, huge TV monitors, and other equipment to accommodate the largest crowd possible. They would be utilizing the twenty-six other halls in the Center too; crowds would watch the trials there on big screen televisions and hope they would be lucky enough to get into the big room the next day. The nun and two monks navigated the crowd of looky-loos separated from the Muslim women by several yards. The monk named Earl led the group to a conference room at the east end of the building and quickly punched the required numbers into the door lock. Earl peaked inside the room and immediately ushered the other monk and nun into the room. The Muslim women hurried through the door after the Christian clergy, and once all were inside, the door bolt was slid into place.

"Well that went nicely," Joe observed.

"Yeah, now let's get changed and get this show on the road," Earl responded.

The group quickly stripped off their outer disguises and placed them neatly out of the eye of the camera and set up for the taping. The interview lasted the usual five minutes but the subject matter was not on the normal topic of salvation through repentance. With the glittering letters ICC Jerusalem behind them, moderated by Marilyn, the Two Witnesses spoke to their audience about the trials that were to begin the next day. Knowing, from reports on TV, that the Bethlehem internment camp where their fellow Resisters were being held had been outfitted with hundreds of TV monitors days earlier to quiet riots, the Prophets spoke directly to the captive Elect.

"Remember what Jesus told you in the Great Book of Mark in chapter 13, you are not to think about what you will say when you are put on trial, but let the Holy Spirit speak through you," Zeke said.

"Yes, and remember what Mark said in chapter 21—they can't harm one hair on your head or they will answer to the Father," the Lawyer added.

When the taping was finished the group put their disguises back on, exited the room, and melded into the growing crowd. No one even knew they had been there, until that evening when their daring act was revealed on television, across the globe!

September 26

The schedule for the trials had been announced early and the world media had been promoting them for over a week, any reduction in coverage now would only show weakness and add to the erosion of Sardinian's support. Once the trials began, it was too late for Sardinian to cancel them. The best he could do was supply the cameras with a stream of fake Resisters professing their allegiance to him, because every time a real Resister slipped through to testify they began speaking in a language that was unique. It was a language understood by everyone who listened without a translator, by everyone in the world. In fact, these Resisters spoke to the listeners in their own language, right down to the local dialect of the region in which they lived. No matter what part of the world the listeners lived, they heard and understood.

By the end of the first day of trials, the elect understood an extraordinary thing was happening right before their eyes. The first few testifiers broke the mold; the cat was out of the bag! News networks all over the world played and replayed the testaments of the true Resisters spoken in the divine language of God. By the time the fake Resisters arrived and were funneled into the trials to tell their lies, many with ears to hear already knew the truth. As the trials drug on some others began to realize what was happening, and the few real Resisters that slipped through and testified reinforced this realization. The Christian Underground had planned well and had planned early for this very event. There were over a hundred moles that infiltrated the New Religion's ranks and were ready to emerge when the time was right. Now, the time had come, and the moles were the first to volunteer for Sardinian's charade at the trials. One by one they were enlisted to pretend to be Resisters testifying of their love and allegiance to Sardinian, but instead turned themselves over to the Holy Spirit.

September 27

Surprisingly, the Prophets and their crew were exercising a freedom they had never expected to achieve and rejoiced in the Glory of the Lord. Their new "outside" attire and the smothering throng of people arriving every day in Jerusalem allowed them to travel around Jerusalem; anytime, anywhere they wished. The group's favorite activity while out among the masses was to watch the news, they stayed abreast of everything that was happening in the world. There were several places that had free Wi-Fi for Earl's laptop, and today they sat in awe and wonder at the images they watched. Sardinian was at the Mt. Zion Cemetery and upon his orders six remains had been exhumed. The remains had been publicly placed on a concrete slab next to each other, and then covered with linin sheets. Sardinian now stood at the head of the remains facing the gathering and spoke.

"You will sing of this day in the eternity, when the Host remembers the day I showed all humans on earth who; I am. A few still have doubts, but all know there is only one that can give life. There is only one who can create life. There is only one that can give life back to the dead. The Father the creator of all! I am that I am!" Sardinian shouted to the crowd. The creature from another place raised his hands above his head and ordered the remains to live again. The crowd began to murmur as the sheets began to move, and then one by one threw off their coverings and stood. Loved ones of the dead rushed to see if their eyes had tricked them. No, they exclaimed their belief! Then, all in attendance worshiped Sardinian.

"He must be feeling the pressure," the Lawyer said after they were safe back in their hideout. "He needed to prove he was God to the world, so he pulled the old "raise the dead" trick. Maybe he thinks he'll get a show in Vegas when this is all over, he is running short on time."

"Running short on time? What do you mean, sir?" Joe asked. The Lawyer smiled that slow long smile Joe had come to admire.

"Revelation chapter 12 verse 12," the old man began. *The devil is come down unto you, having great wrath, because he knoweth that he hath but a short time.*

"The devil, that's who he is! Isn't he?" Joe pleaded for affirmation. The Lawyer nodded yes and lowered his head.

"You already knew that, Joe. Didn't you?" Zeke asked. Joe wasn't sure Zeke expected an answer.

"You know the rest of the story too, don't you?" Zeke continued, obviously posing the question to all three members of the crew. "Of course, you do, you all know the scripture almost as well as I do. It is time to talk about what is going to happen, and how you fit into it."

"But," Joe started, he went no further, he was at a loss for words. "I'm sorry, but who are you guys, anyway?" Joe finally started again. "I mean we've lived with you for a while in this cave. I know you guys are not supernatural, not like Sardinian. I don't mean any disrespect, you both have done some amazing things, but you aren't supernatural. I don't think you are angels either."

"Well, that is correct," Zeke was talking to all three of them. "We are not supernatural…exactly, and we aren't angels yet."

"Well then, who are you? We need to know don't you think?" Marilyn asked. "I believe you are the Two Witnesses, but the scripture never really says who you are. Am I right? Where did you come from? And what do you mean you aren't angels yet?"

The Lawyer answered with a question, "Do you remember what happens to the Two Witnesses?" The group was silent; they knew the answer but did not want to speak. The Lawyer smiled a loving knowing smile before he spoke.

"They die in Jerusalem, and yes, we are ready to become angels. When God raises us from the dead, three and a half days later, we will be changed into our supernatural bodies, we will be the first to be changed, then all will instantly follow us as Paul described in 1 Corinthians. The millennium will have begun.

"Where we came from is a little more complicated," Zeke interjected. "We came from Paradise, what you call Heaven. Just like you did, but we were born a long time ago, this is not our first time here on earth." Zeke could tell from their puzzled looks that they were still confused. "Do you remember the transfiguration of Christ, how afterward He could walk through walls, but at the same time Thomas could feel Jesus's body when he put his hand in the wound in His side? Well, we were with Jesus on that Mountain of Transfiguration, we had our own type of transfigurations when we were each taken to Paradise by God." The Lawyer smiled again. "We have never died in the flesh."

"But in Matthew, it says that Moses and Elijah were on the mountain with Jesus," Earl said questioningly.

"At your service," the two old prophets said in unison, as if they were each part of a fine-tuned two-man vaudeville act from the 1930s.

September 28

The crew had done the math, Yom Kippur, also known as the Day of Atonement was when the trials were scheduled to end and judgement would be administered, and according to the Jewish calendar the day begins at sundown. They were a little less than four days away. The nun and two monks were headed for the International Convention Center, and the two Muslim women were not far behind. Threading their way through the pulsing crowd the group shared the overwhelming guidance of the Holy Spirit. Crossing the street in front of the Jerusalem Central Bus Station they came to the open concrete area at the foot of the stairway leading to the ICC Jerusalem's entrance.

The previous evening, the group discussed the plan for today for hours in the dark of their underground hideout. The Prophets were prepared to die, that was evident, but as they often repeated during their conversations: "God's will be done. It's not our job to bring it on, no more than it was Jesus's job to bring on the crucifixion, but He knew it was coming."

The group had been sitting in silence for a while, finally the Lawyer spoke. "Look, we need to keep on doing what we've been doing, but now we need to go public, out in the open, no more hiding from Lucifer." The crew looked around at each other in the darkness and knew they were all on the same page. Now as they were stripping off their disguises and preparing to tape the entire event, one of them was missing, only one monk's robe fell on to the pile of disguises. The missing monk was not far away, he was just around the corner, sitting on a bench holding his laptop, ready to receive the wireless transmission of their last and final recording. Earl would be entrusted to get the final broadcast from the Prophets to the world after everything was over. Earl could not be captured, he must escape the locust army, so he sat and waited, a lonely monk wearing his dingy blond wig and sun glasses.

It was early in the morning; the trials had not even started yet when Sardinian got the news. The two old men were preaching outside the Convention Center. The two prophets were set up on a little circular piece of grass surrounded by concrete at the entrance to the Center, Sardinian was told. The creature from another dimension blew up with anger and pushed the young woman who had been attending to him away. Pushing everything in his path away, he stormed toward the main entrance of the building, and out on to the landing at the top of the concrete stairway. Below him he could see the growing crowd the two old men were attracting, he could see them and the female news reporter with her camera man.

Why? he wondered; it didn't make any sense, they're coming out of hiding? Two of his trusted lieutenants were beside him, ready to follow his every command.

"What would you have us do, Lord?" one of the lieutenants asked.

"Whatever happens, those two old goats are not to escape," Sardinian commanded as he stepped to the edge of the landing, and in a voice with the power of six trumpets he shouted.

"Stop it! Stop the heresy you are spreading against me! Stop it, I command you!" Sardinian trumpeted as he stood high above the Prophets. "You are nothing but a couple of old heretics, and you are an abomination before the Lord, for it is written; thou shalt not have any other gods before me."

"You are the abomination, Tyrus, you are a blight in the eyes of the one almighty God, Yahveh," Zeke shouted back at the dragon. Sardinian's temper exploded, and he turned to one of his lieutenants and ordered;

"Get that camera! Go! Get it and bring it back to me in pieces!" Sardinian raised his hands to the heavens and shouted, "If I am not the almighty God of heaven and earth, let these men live and go their way in peace, but if they are liars and blasphemers before the Lord; let them be struck down by my divine power!" Suddenly with no warning a booming sound thundered from a white puffy cloud floating above them.

The thunder was accompanied by lightening which emerged from the cloud and struck the two old men dead on the spot. As they lay on the small circle of grass, the hair on their heads still smoking, Marilyn turned and ran into the crowd. A moment later Joe was tackled, kicked, and beaten fiercely, while his camera was stomped into the ground.

"I am that I am," Sardinian trumpeted. "Cordon off the grass area," he ordered.

He turned to his lieutenant and ordered, "Put guards on the area around the clock so the Resisters cannot steal their bodies, like they did with Jesus. I want to see their bodies rot and the maggots devour them." Unknown to Sardinian this order was overheard by a member of the world news media in a nearby group behind him; this reporter was the first to break the story. His network would also set up the "bodies camera," which would transmit the picture of the two dead bodies twenty-four hours a day for the next three and a half days to the world.

One lonely monk pressed through the surging crowd of sight seers, forging his path toward the home of the one person that could help him now. The video his friends had shot today had to make its way onto the internet as soon as possible.

Marilyn watched the attack on Joe from a perch across the street at the bus station, and when it was over, she ventured back across the street, praying Joe survived. In the confusion after his beating, Joe crawled off and hid in some nearby bushes, Marilyn had watched and knew just where to find him. When she got to him, Marilyn saw that Joe was bleeding from the nose, and other places, but no one seemed to be looking for him, or her for that matter. So when Joe had been safely guided around the corner to the same bench Earl had used, she went back for their disguises. In all the confusion no one had seemed to notice the cloths, still in a neat pile over next to a short stem wall where the crew had taken them off. Marilyn scooped the clothing up in a single motion and was gone, no one even looked her way. Now they would at least be able to go outside and find out what was happening. When Joe was ready, Marilyn helped him to his feet and they slowly made their way back to the hideout. Earl made it back to the hideout without a hitch; he assured his friends the video would be on the internet that evening.

Joe wasn't up to it until late that evening but when he was able, the nun and her two monks ventured out into the streets of Jerusalem in search of a good Wi-Fi connection. They had a favorite coffee shop with good Wi-Fi, and they headed in that direction. Early on, Sardinian had decreed in his Law that his converted clergy across the world, who were tending his sheep in many flocks, were to pay nothing for food, shelter, and other services. The nun and her monks, wearing their robes with the embroidered emblem of the Converted Clergy, thanked God for watching over them. It was amazing to the three how every step they took seemed to be planned for them and how they were protected by their Lord.

This morning's events were all over the world media, on every news outlet the group checked, it was the lead story. Surprisingly, the group's video had not emerged yet. All the reporting was using file footage of the ICC Jerusalem along with eye witness accounts of the events. A couple of the networks had begun showing a camera shot from about a hundred yards away, of the circle of grass surrounded by a huge crowd. If you didn't know what you were looking at you might miss them, but the bodies of Mo and Zeke were still there. The other topics dominating the Israeli news that evening was disturbing to say the least. Israel was surrounded on all her borders by a coalition of countries including some Arabian states, China, Syria and Iran, and they were ignoring the stern orders being issued by Sardinian. It seemed they thought the alien had bit off more than he could chew.

On the other side of the world, Russia with China's support had amassed a "million-man army" at the tip of Russia, where it meets the Bering Strait. Military pundits on every news network were speculating what it was about, but the only reasonable explanation was that an attack against the United States was emanate. It looked as though this army planned to attack the United States by land, through Alaska, then down through Canada. When the three clergy were out in public they never spoke to each other, but from time to time Earl would pretend to be praying to communicate his thoughts. His prayers were usually short and repeated a few times to make the point. Tonight, his chant went, "Armageddon, oh, Megiddo. Armageddon, oh, Megiddo."

September 29

The musty subterranean odor of the tunnels encompassed them as they sat in the darkness. The events of yesterday had sunk into their collective beings, it was clear the Two Prophets were dead. Only Earl had not witnessed their demise in person, but he had no doubts about what had happened. Now, after having slept a little, the three disciples of the Two Witnesses were struggling with what their future role was to be. Marilyn believed they should go directly to the trials and try to testify with their brothers and sisters, but Joe pointed out that there was little chance for that to happen if Sardinian's people were aware of who they were.

"They won't let us anywhere near the cameras if they have any idea who we are," Joe insisted.

"We'd have a better chance of winning the lottery than getting on TV at the trials," Earl agree.

After hours of discussion, only one alternative was left to them, they donned their disguises and left their subterranean refuge and went into the streets of Jerusalem in search of news. After hours of observing every bit of information available, the nun and her two monks returned underground.

"Well, it's just like we thought," Joe was the first to speak.

"Yes, there isn't much happening we didn't expect," Earl agreed.

"I'm not sure I agree," Marilyn said. "I was very surprised about the US president's secret message. And are you telling me, you really expected the representative of the European Union to speak out against the Devil? They have turned and ran in the opposite direction for decades every time Jews and Christians have been threatened. And what about our tape making it on to the internet, did you really think the channels would still be open at this point?"

The monks were shocked; the nun had called them on the carpet. "I always had faith in my connections," Earl asserted. "I knew they would get our video out. But what about the president of the United States? What did I miss?"

"Yeah," Joe agreed, "what are you talking about, Marilyn?"

"It's not only what he said, it is what he did. You didn't see him make the sign of the cross on his lips before he started speaking? I mean, he didn't make a big deal of it, it was subtle." She was met with blank stares. "He's not Catholic, he's evangelical, and you guys know they don't cross themselves. Besides that, he said he had seen some video that he found very disturbing and would be commenting on it after he had a chance to examine it closer."

"Yeah?" The monks were a little slow today.

"What video do you think he was talking about?" She asked. "And don't you remember me telling you about the Christian Underground adopting the crossing of the lips to show their alliance and support for all true believers of all religions across the globe? Sort of like the fish was back in biblical days."

Their silence was her answer; they obviously were not good listeners.

"Guys," Marilyn scolded, "he knows the truth, he's with us. It's our video he saw. He saw Sardinian kill the Two Witnesses! Think about it! We saw the video on the internet tonight. He must have seen it too. The other big surprise of today was that there was absolutely no response to our video. Right? I bet you two didn't see that one coming. The world is afraid of Sardinian, everyone is afraid to speak out against him because he is so powerful!"

The guys looked back in the direction of her shadowy figure with no response.

"Really? You don't get it?" She taunted them. "He knows, he believes, and I don't think the President of the United States is afraid."

The phone on the desk in the Oval Office rang, and the President answered it.

"They are here, sir," his secretary said.

"Send them in please," he responded.

Since day 1, the situation inside the White House grounds had been markedly different than in the rest of the District of Columba, in fact it was different than most any other place in the world, except for every other piece of ground owned by the United States of America. The President, while publicly acknowledging Sardinian, banned him and his followers access to those facilities based on National Security concerns. He publicly stated that he would need to investigate the situation before making any decision. He completely denied access to all sites except ones normally used by the public, such as National Parks and Monuments. The reaction in the beginning was one of shock, but by this point in time, a growing number of Americans were grateful for his actions. Unlike Israel, the United States had not allowed Sardinian's bracelets to be used, on the basis it would be a violation of Americans' civil rights. Because of the President's actions the Christian Underground in America was much larger and more developed than in Israel. In the beginning everyone expected Sardinian to quash the President for his insolence, but now over five months later, the President was still investigating, and the White House was still a sanctuary.

The door to the Oval Office opened and Bishop Hayden and his confessor, Father Ramirez, were greeted by the President. The right sleeve of both of their robes bore the embroidered emblem of the Converted Clergy, but as they faced one another, they each crossed their lips.

"Gentlemen," the President addressed the clergymen, "thank you for risking the trip here, but I need your help." The two priests were all ears. "I'm going to make an address in a few hours that will be played from one end of the globe to the other, and I want to get it right. My contact with the Underground tells me I can trust the two of you, I need your advice. Will you pray with me?"

The President extended his arms and they joined hands. "Dear Lord, please forgive us our sins, and give us the strength to do your will. Please give us the wisdom dear Lord, to know your will and the courage to stand strong. Please guide us dear Lord in our time of danger and deliver us into your arms. We ask this in your son Jesus's precious name. Amen."

September 30

The nun and her monks had been out on the streets all morning, and the news was buzzing everywhere they went, all they had to do was listen. The streets were alive with conversations, wondering what the American president was going to say. Most news outlets were saying the US government would be offering to return to the World Peace Conference and accept Sardinian as the world's supreme leader. Many pointed out that the President had remained open-minded and had been investigating and deliberating on the matter for months. They believed the United States would join the coalition against Israel and assure their own place in the Eternity. Many pointed out that the million-man army amassed just across the Bering Strait must have influenced his decision. Others argued that no one was crazy enough to go against the almighty God of heaven and earth.

The nun and monks had discussed the situation late into the evening the night before, and before going to sleep, they prayed to the Father for guidance in Jesus's name. Marilyn pointed out to Joe and Earl; "We have never really turned this thing over to the Father as a group. I think we need to do that, and if we do I believe He will show us exactly what to do." Now as they navigated the streets of the Holy City the Holy Spirit was in control. They had a plan, and they were driven by the Spirit.

The latest event making news was the formation of a tremendous crowd that was building around the bodies of the two old dead men. Information had leaked that the Christian Underground expected the two prophets to rise from the dead at the end of three and a half days; the story went viral. A bottom corner of every news network's broadcast picture was now dedicated to a live shot of the circular grass area where the two men's bodies still lay unattended on the ground. A clock at the bottom of the picture showed how much time was left before the three and a half days would expire. The crowd around the bodies swelled to fill the adjoining streets for blocks, and it was becoming a party. Sardinian had decreed that when the two old men failed to come back to life, it would bring an end to this ridiculous Jesus-based resistance. His swarm of supporters cheered his statement, they were giddy with joy over the death of the two prophets, whose videos had tormented them for months. Furthermore, Sardinian ordered a six-day world celebration to follow the official declaration of permanent death of his two advisories. Sardinian declared that at the end of the celebration he would begin moving souls into the Eternity. His followers were starting the party early, in a few hours the entire city would be in a quagmire.

It was almost sundown in Jerusalem, signaling both the end of that day and the beginning of the next. It would also begin a twenty-four-hour count down leading to the beginning of Yon Kipper; the Day of Atonement. The three friends knew the clock was ticking, they also knew it was running on God's time. The President's announcement would be at eight pm Washington, DC time, that would be in about eight hours. The three clergymen headed back to get some rest, tomorrow promised to be a long day. The Spirit was surging in the three disciples of the Two Witnesses and they were on a path guided from above. They knew where they had to go tomorrow but had no idea why.

October 1

The three were back on the streets an hour before the President's announcement, and restlessly waited for the highly anticipated broadcast. The President of the United States began his address to the world a little after 8:00 p.m. Washington, DC, time, which was a little after 3:00 a.m. in Jerusalem. Amazingly the streets of the Holy City were packed at that hour, as if it were a Saturday afternoon; anticipation was through the roof. The nun and her two monks waited patiently to hear the President's words, and when they finally had been spoken their impact was profound. For fear of exposing themselves by losing control of their emotions, they hurried back underground silently.

He would deliver his message sitting behind his desk in the Oval Office. He would speak directly into the one camera in front of him, and now leaning back and stretching in his desk chair, he found he wasn't nervous at all. The President would have rather had it over, there was no doubt of that, but he wasn't nervous. The sound of the door opening got his attention, it would be five minutes until the broadcast would begin, and the TV people had left the room. He looked toward the door, it was his wife. He was surprised because he knew the hoops, she must have had to jump through to get into his office without his permission.

"Hello, darling, is everything all right?" the President asked. "You know I'm about to make a pretty important speech." The President knew she was aware of this announcement, they had talked in length about it earlier in the day. He had bared his soul to her and explained he was concerned that Sardinian's motives might not be in the United States's best interest.

"It's very important, dear, you know I wouldn't intrude if it weren't."

"Well, what is it? I only have a couple of minutes," the President inquired patiently.

"I talked to Reverend Walker this afternoon after you and I talked, and he is very concerned about what you are going to say," the First Lady informed him.

"You told him what I confided in you?" The President's temper flashed. "That wasn't just between you and me, that was as top secret as it gets! Damn it, Liz."

"Don't speak to me in that tone, you know the Reverend's congregation makes up over half of Sardinian's Christian converts across this country. His influence with Sardinian is probably the only reason he hasn't come in here and taken you out. You can't stand up to him you aren't strong enough, this is going to be like poking him in the eye with a stick."

"You are wrong, dear, I don't have to stand up to him, I have God to do that, now get out of here before I have you removed by Security. How would that look to all your friends there in Reverend Walker's congregation?" The TV people were coming back into the room. The President had seen the First Lady's total conversion coming, but now he knew it was official. Over thirty years of marriage, working in their local church the entire time, her betrayal was disheartening. He had tried to talk to her but what did he know about it compared to Reverend Walker?

"Two minutes, Mr. President," the producer said.

The President pointed at the door and gave his wife a sharp glare. The First Lady turned abruptly and left the room. The President leaned back in his chair, took a deep breath, and let his mind clear. *Don't premeditate what you are going to say*, he thought.

"Thirty seconds." It was the producer; the President snapped back. He stretched and sat up straight in his chair. The producer was holding up five fingers, then four, then three, then two, then one, then the President of the United States felt the Holy Spirit engulf him and he began to speak.

"I want to talk to you tonight about something of ultimate importance to mankind, but first I want you watch a video, so everyone knows what we are talking about."

The screen went black for just a moment then the image of the Two Witnesses preaching in front of ICC Jerusalem came into view. They were warning the crowd about being deceived and quoted scripture to back up their statements. Then the camera panned up the concrete staircase to where Sardinian was standing and captured the entire scene. Every word and action were documented on video, Joe had done an excellent job, he got everything from Sardinian's temper tantrum to his execution of the Two Witnesses. At the end of the video the image of the President returned to the screen and he began to speak.

"I am here tonight to declare to the world that the United States of America cannot condone Sardinian's actions and I am calling the perpetrator out for what he is, a fake, a phony, and a fraud. But most importantly, he is a criminal, you just witnessed him murder two innocent men. This man is not my God!" The President spoke for a little over fifteen minutes and covered several issues the Christian Underground had been trying to get out into the news media all day. The President asked why any all-powerful supreme being would be killing innocent people. The President agonized over the millions of young people mostly girls that had virtually disappeared into the metallic disks never to be seen by their families again. He pointed out that Sardinian hadn't delivered on many of his promises, and certainly hadn't given any proof he could take anyone into the Eternity. The President ended by quoting Saint Paul, 1 Corinthians 15:52:

*"In a moment, in the twinkling of an eye, at the
last trump: for the trumpet shall sound, and the*

dead shall be raised incorruptible, and we shall be changed."

"Changed, the instant the Lord returns," the President said emphatically, "has anyone changed into their spiritual bodies lately? No? Has anyone heard that final Trumpet sound? Have those that have gone before us been raised from the dead? Well then friends, God hasn't returned yet. God bless America! God bless the whole world! God bless you all, please pray for me, please pray for us all. Good night."

Alberto the producer, who had been born and raised as a child in Italy, was in a state of shock. He wasn't alone; television translators all over the world were stunned along with the rest of the non-English speaking world. Everyone everywhere heard the President's speech in their own language; translators had the night off.

October 2

The three counterfeit clergy were out on the street early; the Day of Atonement, Yom Kippur, would begin at sundown. They were on the clock, time was running out. According to the tickers at the bottom of every news feed across the world, they had about twelve hours left. Disguised in their Sardinian approved garb, they would ride the bus to Bethlehem for free, what they would do then they left to the Lord. The group caught the Egged bus at the Damascus Gate and headed south on sixty.

The President received an on-slot of messages, mostly negative about his speech of the night before, but some praised his courage. Satellite images showed that the million-man army had moved across the Bering Strait and was now staging on American soil. The noose around Israel was also tightening and their enemies were ready to pounce. He believed he needed to be patient, he felt he needed to let the Lord do His work. His military advisors were beside themselves, the picture they were painting was dark. The Russians and their allies would be moving across Alaska and down into Canada unchecked.

"Canada isn't going to try to stop them," his advisors told him, "they will run in the other direction as fast as they can."

"We need to attack them now with everything we have," the president was told. A couple advisors even favored the use of nuclear weapons. "We need to destroy them now, Mr. President," one general almost yelled. "Every minute you waste is going to cost American lives, sir." The general's volume seemed to excite everyone in the room except the President.

"Put our missile defenses on high alert and notify the Air Force to be ready at a moment's notice, general." The President's order was met with silent disagreement from the general, which was evident to all. "Keep me updated every ten minutes, and sooner if developments demand."

"But, sir, you don't understand..." the general began, but the President cut him off.

"Mac, you know I respect your opinion greatly, now please follow my orders." The small disgruntled group left the Oval Office.

The President had made up his mind; this was in God's hands.

The bus ride took a little under forty minutes, there didn't seem to be much traffic on the road. The nun and the two monks had talked extensively the night before, and much of the conversation centered around a shared dream they each had. There were a few differences in their dreams, but they were unified on where they needed to go, the big question was what they were to do when they got to Bethlehem. Again, they knew exactly where in Bethlehem they needed to go but were driven by the biggest mystery of all from their shared dream. At the high point of the dream in all three versions, they were standing in front of the huge doors at the entrance to the Church of the Nativity. Then the dream ended, and they were left with the mystery of who the three were with; it was two handsome young men in flowing white robes. One of the two handsome young men was just about to speak, then they each woke up.

The trials had been going on for about an hour, and Sardinian and his six liements listened patiently to the praise this current

"Resister" was pouring on them now that he had seen the light. They had not experienced a real Resister since early yesterday afternoon; perhaps the rumors of terrible physical punishment doled out to the real Christians who successfully slipped through Sardinian's screeners were working. Sardinian had been carefully structuring and leaking gruesome stories of torturer administered to all who would dare cross their creator.

Or perhaps there are no more infiltrators left, Sardinian thought.

Sardinian's first inclination had been to immediately take the insolent Christians off the stage the minute they started testifying in that damnable tongue, but he resisted the urge. Each person was only allowed six minutes and there weren't that many, so he let them talk. The worst thing was he knew the world was hearing them, because of that damnable tongue. The current testifier was finishing up and Sardinian noticed the next speaker was a beautiful woman in her late thirties.

A little old, Sardinian thought, *but still…she's a knockout. I wonder how she slipped through the others' hands…I know where she'll be tonight,* he thought, smiling at her broadly as the woman stepped to the microphone.

"Praise Yahveh, the Lord Almighty! We are nearing the moment when the Lord Jesus will return," the woman spoke slow and clear, looking directly into the camera, speaking in that language everyone understood. Sardinian released a deep frustrated sigh.

The nun and her two monks rounded the corner and were looking down the long wide concrete pavilion leading to the entrance of the Church of the Nativity. The pavilion was almost deserted, every place in Bethlehem was deserted, it seemed everyone had gone to Jerusalem for the big party. The trio was mesmerized by the two lone figures standing at the entrance of the church. Standing there beside the huge doors watching them, were two young men in flowing white robes. As the three approached the figures they searched their memories unsuccessfully trying to identify them.

As they drew near the two men one of them spoke, "I'm glad to see you made it." They knew the voice, but the face was unfamiliar to them. "Yeah, I guess the traffic wasn't too bad, huh?" The other young man said. The trio was in shock, they couldn't grasp what was happening, the voices they heard belonged to their two dead friends, the Prophets.

"What the...?" was all Marilyn could muster, the other two remained silent.

"We understand how this might be a little surprising to you," the taller one said.

"Mo!" Earl finally found his voice. "How? What?" There were no words for the situation.

The time had come in their relationships, after the two prophets had revealed their identity to their three friends, that everyone agreed "the Lawyer" should no longer be Moses's handle. Earl quickly shortened it to Mo, reflecting the close friendship they had cultivated. Joe chose Moses to address the man, but Marilyn had clung to Sir when addressing him. Oddly, Zeke on the other hand seemed to still work for everyone. Later that evening, Joe could contain himself no longer, the question had been festering in all their minds, Joe just blurt it out first.

"So if you are Elijah, how did you get the nick name Zeke?" Joe asked. The old prophet smiled a wily smile before he answered.

"Well," Zeke began, "interesting that you ask. It's kind of a funny story actually." Mo was beaming; he had evidently heard the story before. "As you can imagine, we were kind of oddities when we first arrived in Paradise. Enoch was the first; I guess you could say he paved the way for the rest of us 'Transfigurationists.'" Everyone smiled at that one.

"Everyone knew we were around, but nobody paid us much attention," Zeke continued. "So one day I ran into Peter, who I had only met once before in this Heaven Age, and he introduced me to some angels. He introduced me to them as Zeke. You know he fancies himself as a bit of a comedian. Anyway, he explained to the angels that my real name was Ezekiel, but he calls me Zeke. Of course, everyone knew his mistake and thought it was the funniest thing ever, so the nickname stuck, and I've been Zeke ever since."

None of them knew for sure, if the story was true or if Zeke was just putting them on.

The morning was fading into the afternoon and the deployment was moving on without a hitch. The Russian commander was aware of the air-cover he was being provided, and he knew there were two or three submarines just off shore that were there for his operation's protection. Still, he was uneasy; this was an act of aggression against the super-power of all super-powers. He was quite sure he would be attacked at any moment. Half of his tanks and support vehicles were rolling; they would form a safety buffer for his troop, some of whom were on foot. The invasion force was so large Russia didn't have enough transport vehicles to accommodate the number of foot soldiers moving into this hostile territory. The rest of his tanks and support vehicles would follow the troops, covering their rear. He hoped his superiors knew what they were doing, this whole thing seemed crazy to him.

"Okay, so if you two are Mo and Zeke," Earl asked, "what happened to the old you?"

"Well, it's a difficult thing to explain," Mo began, "but I'll try. You saw Sardinian kill us, right? I mean I wasn't watching you, guys, but I figure you were watching us."

"Yes, we saw," Joe affirmed.

"Well, we died. I told you before that we hadn't died in the flesh like most people, so now we have, and here we are in our spiritual bodies. We are angels and it is wonderful." Mo smiled.

"And," Zeke added, "in a few hours, through the power of Almighty God, our souls will return back into our old flesh bodies for a short while."

"And," Mo finished, "after we take care of a little business with the Old Serpent, we will be changed into our incorruptible spiritual bodies with all of you when our Lord Jesus returns to earth." The nun and the two monks were mesmerized by the eternal truth of God and engulfed by the Holy Spirit.

"But first we have work to do," Moses brought them back to the moment. "We need to give aid and comfort to our sisters and brothers who have been imprisoned here. Come on my friends, you are going to love the new powers we have discovered in our spiritual bodies."

The phone on the President's desk rang and he answered it. A few moments later, Bishop Hayden, Father Ramirez, and several other clerics entered the Oval Office. Shortly after the President's speech, his contact with the Christian Underground called. She had been contacted by several members who said they now trusted the President and wanted to help. This meeting was set up. A wide range of denominations were represented, and the President found comfort in their support.

"Gentlemen and ladies, thank you for coming, please pray with me." He reached out his arms and the entire group joined hands. "Dear Lord, please forgive us our sins, and please, dear Lord, bestow your Wisdom upon us. We ask for your protection dear Lord and pledge our love to You. And please give us strength, dear Lord, in accomplishing your will. We ask in Jesus's name. Amen.

"Friends I need your help, just as you need mine. We need to strengthen our resolve against this Monster, and I want you to lead me in Scripture, so we can all understand what's happening."

The nun, two monks, and their angels walked the few blocks over across Manger Street to the open area where Sardinian had interned the Elect. The camp was protected by forty fully armed soldiers who had pledged their eternal allegiance to Sardinian. As the two angels and their friends approached the entrance Zeke and Mo raised their arms high in the air, and the weapons of every solider fell from their hands. The forty-armed soldiers were frozen in space and time, just to insure everyone's safety until Jesus's return.

Zeke's voice was like a bull-horn, "Will all doctors and anyone with medical experience please come up here."

"We need to care for the sick and injured," Mo was telling the disciples. "We need to take care of them and get them fed, they are still in their flesh bodies!" He was smiling widely. And so, the medical people were assembled to help the sick and injured, physically and psychologically, and all serious cases were brought to the Angels and they healed the people. Before long, a few hundred more angels showed up in the largest shinning disk any of them had seen yet. The medical attention continued for hours, there were over six thousand people interned. The angels fed the crowd with the best pizza anyone could ever remember tasting. Those that didn't like pizza were offered either tacos or fish with loaves of bread. After lunch, the multitude was ushered into the enormous vehicle. Amazingly, after everyone was aboard, there was still plenty of room for more.

The man in charge of the forces amassed around the country of Israel, still didn't believe anything would come of this maneuver. The military action had put pressure not only on Israel but also on the alien and the commander had been sure a negotiated agreement would be reached. When the order came he couldn't believe it, it was suicide! He called the Intelligence Center to get their read on the situation; it was real. He gave the order, there was no turning back now. The tanks moved forward and began to fire, and the sound of the ballistic missiles firing off into the air rang in his ears.

It was like the ship never moved, but in seconds, the hatch opened again, and they were at the Temple Mount. The occupants of the craft emptied out on to the open area around the Dome of the Rock and flowed out into the area known as Solomon's Stables. The two Angels put their arms around their disciples and comforted them.

"We must go," Zeke said, "but we will see you soon in the millennium. You must wait here for the coming of our Lord, our Brethren will protect you. We are so blessed, this is an amazing moment in time." Zeke gave them that wryly smile that always reassured them.

As the ship rose from the ground a booming voice they knew well spoke to the crowd. "Bless you all, wait here for the coming of the Lord, He will not tarry long. Do not fear, you are protected by the Living God!" One moment the ship was there slowly lifting off the ground, the next moment it was nowhere to be seen.

The activity around the grass circle at the ICC Jerusalem was at a high pitch, Sardinian's people had taken control. They forced the crowd back from the barriers and television crews took their place. The tickers were down to minutes now, and you could cut the excitement with a knife. Sardinian had announced earlier in the day that one half an hour needed to be added to the time remaining before the permanent death decree would be pronounced. The news networks had scrambled and added thirty minutes to their tickers, there was now less than five minutes left.

As the seconds ticked away, the crowd's exhilaration grew. Sardinian had cleared a secure space at the top of the stairway, leading to the entrance of the ICC Jerusalem, above the prophets' bodies. Now, Sardinian exited the building and stood at the edge of the platform, looking down on the people and the dead bodies. As the last tick of the clock spent itself a hush came over the crowd. Sardinian raised his arms to the heavens and spoke.

"As you can see with your own eyes, these two reprobates are dead, their bodies decay and are stinking. There can be no doubt the heretical Christian belief is based on a lie." The sound of thunder was heard far off and dust began to invade the air.

The thunder was deafening, and the Russian commander lost all communications. The earth was shaking, and the dust was suffocating, on the other side of the world the man in charge of the forces surrounding Israel was experiencing the same thing. When the stones started falling they were only small pebbles, stinging the people they hit but not much more. Within seconds, the pebbles had turned to stones and then the stones turned into boulders. The destruction was devastating; the loss of life was enormous. The impact of the hail of boulders was felt a thousand miles away in Canada and shook the foundations of Jerusalem in Israel. The destruction in the Holy City was breath taking, but seven thousand people stood upon the Temple Mount and watched untouched.

Then, coming from the east was a beautiful growing sound, it was a trumpet, the heavenly sound of a trumpet. And then a light, a glowing growing light that was so beautiful it was indescribable.

Postscript

It is sometimes difficult to imagine how the end time events fulfilling God's prophesies will roll out in this world of flesh. As I said before, I have the same information you have available concerning these events, the Word of God and an awareness of world events. I can, however, tell you this for sure; Satan and his buddies will return (Mathew 25:41), and I think sooner rather than later. I can also assure you they will come in vehicles. Scripture is very clear on that, read the first chapter of Ezekiel. And they will have supernatural powers and abilities like we have never seen (Daniel 8:25). And as I tried to subtly portray, the fallen angels have a physical attraction to the female gender of our species that they cannot seem to control. The evidence of this can be found throughout the Old Testament as well as in the New Testament. In Genesis, we find this attraction the angels have for women is what caused their downfall in the first place, and eventually brought on Noah's flood. The flood was meant to kill the abominable offspring of these supernatural beings and the daughters of Adam; Noah's family was the only group that had not been tainted by these perverts (Genesis 6:1–9).

In the New Testament, in a passage that makes some modern-day women uncomfortable, Paul makes it clear the Fallen Angels are a threat. Many mistakenly interpret Paul's message in 1 Corinthians as a "putdown" of women, as it states,

> *For the man is not of the woman; but the woman of the man.* (11:8)

> *Neither was the man created for the woman; but the woman for the man.* (11:9)

I understand how this might sound to a liberated modern woman, but if you put it in context, all it is saying is that the gift of human reproduction comes to us through woman, and in the description given us of creation woman was formed from man. It is difficult to look beyond the veil but Jesus taught that there will not be male and female in the eternity. I believe that is why all angels in the Bible are described as young males, remember, the fallen angels reproduced with the women of Noah's time and produced giants. So if you open your mind to God's Wisdom you may begin to see that what Paul is really talking about; the attraction the angels have for women.

> *For this cause ought the women to have power on her head because of the angels.* (11:10)

As we have seen, the fallen angels are very attracted to female humans, and if you don't keep the power of Christ over you and in your mind (*on her head*) they will have you when they return. Paul is talking about using the covering of Christ, the Gospel Armor, to protect yourself against the sexual on-slot of the fallen angels. That is what Paul, in the previous verse 7, means where he says men should not cover their heads. Men should not have to worry about the angels being attracted to them; that would be an even greater perversion.

One big problem those that believe the human race was started and nurtured along by extraterrestrials from outer space have is the Bible, as well as the Koran, and many other "holy books" from across the globe. Let's just concentrate on the Bible; if humans were started and nurtured along by extraterrestrials it would mean that aliens from outer space lied to the Israelites and made up stories about everything, for thousands of years, from the Creation of our world to the Resurrection of Christ. While using their extraterrestrial space crafts and other technology to affect the history of man, such as in the parting of the Red Sea, they would also have spread an untrue doctrine of forgiveness of sins through repentance, and salvation through Christ's death on the cross. Why would they do that? Why wouldn't they just tell us the truth? Why wouldn't they just say we are a product of their experimentation? Wouldn't that have been easier to accept than stories about angels and other powerful supernatural beings from another dimension?

Personally, I think the reason so many people today accept the idea of extraterrestrials coming to earth and being responsible for us is that it is easier for them to believe than having faith in the supernatural. For them to visualize that mankind is the work of supernatural powers beyond anything that exists on earth is harder to believe than believing in aliens from outer space. It seems belief in physical possibilities comes easier than belief in spiritual possibilities.

I'd like you to consider what has happen over the past fifty plus years; the technological advancements that have been made are mind-blowing. Fifty years ago, we had no smart phones or personal computers of any kind. Since man first stepped foot on the moon our everyday lives have changed dramatically, from smart televisions and what we watch for entertainment to the ways we travel. In the 1960s, you may have had three or less TV channels you could watch on a black and white TV. Perhaps cars and airplanes have evolved even more. Everything we use in our everyday lives has evolved at a whirlwind speed, from things so common today such as microwave ovens and modern air conditioning, to the emergence of artificial intelligence and robotics. Sometimes it is hard to imagine what is right around the corner, but there is one thing that has not advanced at all. Even during a time when science has been continually reaching out to make contact with life forms of any kind, we have no more knowledge about UFOs or extraterrestrials than we did in 1968. How can that be if the universe is teaming with life and extraterrestrials have been visiting our planet for thousands of years? With our advances in technology it seems impossible that we wouldn't have made contact of some kind.

Finally, I'd like to return to the basics, back to the number one law given to mankind. It is, in fact, exactly what this book has been about, you can find it in Exodus 20:3, you may know it as the First Commandment:

"Thou shalt have no other gods before me."

It has always been the flash point, from the beguilement of Eve in the Garden, to the final temptation by Satan at the end of the Millennium, Satan wants to be God, and he wants you to worship him. The Temptation of Christ, as is recorded in the fourth chapter of Matthew, was Satan's attempt to get Jesus to worship a false god, to violate the First Commandment.

In this whirlwind modern time, it is difficult not to put worldly things before God. In fact, without a lot of prayer and serious inward examination, it is very difficult. It must become a top priority for modern Christians; enjoy God's gifts but understand from where they came and don't make them the top priority in your life. In these dangerous End Times, we need to tune into God's will and lead our lives accordingly.

The end.

References and Sources

Angel, P. (2006) THE MYSTERIOUS MEGATLITHS OF NEW ENGLAND. Article: OOPARTS & ANCIENT HIGH TECHNOLOGY. http://s8int.com/page38.html.

Abrams, A. A MYSTERIOUS SARCOPHAGUS THAT MAY NOT HAVE BEEN OPENED IN 2,000 YEARS WAS FOUND IN EGYPT. Article: Time. http://time.com/5337768/sarcophagus-alexandria-egypt-mystery/.

Bristowe, S. SARGON THE MAGNIFICENT. Burnaby, BC: Association of the Covenant People.

Bullinger, E. (reprint of 1893 ed.) THE WITNESS OF THE STARS. Grand Rapids: Kregel Publications.

Cahn, J. (2012) THE HARBINGER: THE ANCIENT MYSTERY THAT HOLDS THE SECRET OF AMERICA'S FUTURE. Lake Mary: FrontLine.

Cahn, J. (2014) THE MYSTERY IF THE SHEMITAH. Lake Mary: FrontLine.

Capt, E. (1986). A STUDY IN PYRAMIDOLOGY. Muskogee: Artisan Sales.

Capt, E. (1985) MISSING LINKS DISCOVERED IN ASSYRIAN TABLETS. Muskogee: Artisan Sales.

Capt, E. (1979). STONEHENGE AND DRUIDISM. Muskogee: Artisan Sales.

Capt, E. (1999). THE GREAT PYRAMID DECODED. Muskogee: Artisan Sales.

Childress, D. (2000) TECHNOLOGY OF THE GODS. Kempton: Adventures Unlimited Press.

Childress, D. ARK OF GOD. Kempton: Adventures Unlimited Press.

Corso, P. (1997) THE DAY AFTER ROSWELL. New York: Gallery Books.

Dahl, T. DID THE DENISOVANS BECOME THE LEGENDARY GIANTS IN THE INDIAN MOUNDS OF THE USA? Article: terje@sydhav.no: http://www.sydhav.no/giants/denisova_giants_usa.htm.

Dewhurst, R. THE ANCIENT GIANTS WHO RULLED AMERICA. Article: GRAHAM HANCOCK. https://grahamhancock.com/dewhurstr1/.

Dowell, C. (2007). THE STONE BALLS IN ZAVIDOVICI, BOSNIA. Article: CIRCULAR TIMES, An International Networking Educational Institute. http://www.robertschoch.net/Bosnia%20Spherical%20Stone%20Balls%20Semir%20Osmanagic%20Pyramid%20Colette%20Dowell%20CT.htm.

Downing, B (1973) THE BIBLE AND FLYING SAUCERS. Great Britain: Sphere Books

Geggel, L. (2015). ANCIENT MONOLITH SUGGESTS HUMANS LIVED ON NOW-UNDERWATER ARCHIPELAGO. Article: LIVESCIENCE. https://www.livescience.com/51848-monolith-sicilian-channel.html.

Harris, K. (2013) A GIANT MYSTERY; 18 STRANGE GIANT SKELETONS FOUND IN WISCONSIN; SONS OF GOD; MEN OF RENOWN. SOTT. https://www.sott.net/article/256712-A-giant-mystery-18-strange-giant-skeletons-found-in-Wisconsin-Sons-of-god-Men-of-renown.

Haupt, R. (2015) THE STONE SPHERES OF COSTA RICA. Article: SKEPTOID. https://skeptoid.com/episodes/4452.

Hoopes, J. (2016) DEBUNKING THE "MYSTERY" OF THE COSTA RICA STONE BALLS. Article; WORLD-MYSTERIES. http://www.world-mysteries.com/guest-authors/stone-balls-spheres-costa-rica/.

Ivan. WHO PUT THE MYSTERIOUS MONOLITH ON PHO-BOS? Article: Ancient CODE. https://www.ancient-code.com/the-mysterious-monolith-on-phobos-who-put-it-there/.

Kluger, J. WHY NASA IS RIGHT TO HIRE A 'PLANETARY PRO-TECTION OFFICER'. Article: TIME. http://time.com/4884419/nasa-planetary-protection-officer/.

Jensen J. SUPER-MEGALITHIC SITE FOUND IN RUSSIA; NAT-URAL OR MAN-MANDE? Article: MYSTERIOUS UNI-VERSE. https://mysteriousuniverse.org/2014/02/super-megalithic-site-found-in-russia-natural-or-man-made/.

JNTO, the official tourism website of Japan. TOMB OF EMPEROR NINTOKU. Article web-site: https://www.japan.travel/en/spot/19/.

Line, P. GIANTS IN THE LAND: AN ASSESSMENT OF GIGAN-TOPITHECUS AND MEGANTHROPUS. Article: Creation.com. https://creation.com/giants-in-the-land-an-assessment-of-gigantopithecus-and-meganthropus.

MacPherson, D. (1975) THE INCREDIBLE COVER-UP, Medford: Omega Publications.

May, A. (2017) NASA IS HIRING A PLANETARY PROTECTION OFFICER TO PROTECT EARTH FROM ALIEN HARM. Article: USA TODAY. https://www.usatoday.com/story/news/nation-now/2017/08/02/nasa-hiring-planetary-protection-officer-protect-earth-alien-harm/532221001/.

Metaxas, E. (2014). MIRACLES. New York: Penguin Group.

Nield, D. (2018) A MASSIVE, BLACK SARCOPHAGUS HAS BEEN UNEARTHED IN EGYPT, AND NOBODY KNOWS WHO'S INSIDE. Science Alert. https://www.sciencealert.com/huge-mystery-sarcophagus-unearthed-in-egypt-alexandria.

Parker, C. (2007) THERE WERE GIANTS IN THOSE Days: A LOOK BACK AT TWO GIANT STORIES REPORTED IN THE RECENT PAST... Article: OOPARTS & ANCIENT HIGH TECHNOLOGY. http://s8int.com/phile/giants22.html.

Rogers, SA. 7 MYSTERIOUS & MONUMENTAL MAN-MADE WONDERS OF AMERICA. Article: WEB URBANIST. https://weburbanist.com/2012/05/21/7-mysterious-monumental-man-made-wonders-of-america/.

Schneider, K. (2015) JAPAN'S ATLANTIS? THE UNSOLVED UNDERWATER MYSTERY. Article: World Travel Asia. https://www.news.com.au/travel/world-travel/asia/japans-atlantis-the-unsolved-underwater-mystery/news-story/3ef525273ae-cf8e9774110e961b2f6cd.

Shah A. the different ancient sites of the world and their mysterious alignment! Article: ANCIENTEXPLORERS. https://ancientexplorers.com/blogs/news/the-different-ancient-sites-of-the-world-and-their-mysterious-alignment.

Snyder, M. (2014) NEWLY FOUND MEGALITHIC RUNINS IN RUSSIA CONTAIN THE LARGEST BLOCKS OF STONE EVER DISCOVERED. Article: INFOWARS. https://www.infowars.com/newly-found-megalithic-ruins-in-russia-contain-the-largest-blocks-of-stone-ever-discovered/.

Staff. Mysterious alignment of ancient sites of the world. Article: Unexplained Mysteries. https://coolinterestingstuff.com/mysterious-alignment-of-ancient-sites-of-the-world.

Staff. (2010) MYSTERIOUS STONE SPHERES IN COSTA RICA INVESTIGATED. Article: ScienceDaily. https://www.sciencedaily.com/releases/2010/03/100322143217.htm.

Staff. MYSTIC PLACES. WORLD-MYSTERIES: http://www.world-mysteries.com/mystic-places/.

Staff. THE EXCEPTIONAL KOKINO OBSERVATORY: ANCIENT MEGALITHIC SITE, HOLY MOUNTAIN. Article: Ancient Origins. https://www.ancient-origins.net/ancient-places-europe/exceptional-kokino-observatory-ancient-megalithic-site-holy-mountain-004070

Staff. (2017) YONAGUNI MONUMENT, JAPAN: ANCIENT UNDERWATER "PYRAMID." Article: MATRIXDISCLO-SURE. https://www.matrixdisclosure.com/yonaguni-ancient-underwater-pyramid/.

Strong, J. (1980). STRONG'S EXHAUSTIVE CONCORDANCE OF THE BIBLE. Massachusetts: Hendrickson.

Sutherland, A. MYSTERY OF ANCIENT SARCOPHAGI IN EGYPT. Article: AncientPages.com. http://www.ancientpages.com/2015/08/26/mystery-ancient-sarcophagi-egypt/.

Tellinger, M. (2010) DISCOVERING THE OLDEST MAN-MADE STRUCTURES ON EARTH. Article: Wendag Website. https://www.bibliotecapleyades.net/sumer_anunnaki/esp_sumer_annunaki34.htm.

AND the Edge: http://www.edgemagazine.net/2010/10/oldest-man-made-structures/.

Tellinger, M. (2010). THE OLDEST MAN-MADE STRUCTURES ON EARTH. Articles: Megalithomania. http://www.megalithomania.co.uk/michaelarticle.html.

Von Daniken, E. (1999). CHARIOTS OF THE GODS. New York: Berkley.

Von Daniken, E. (1970). GODS FROM OUTER SPACE. New York: Putnam.

Walton, T. (1996) FIRE IN THE SKY Boston: Da Capo Press.

Ward, B. (1996). NOSTRADAMUS THE MAN WHO SAW TOMORROW. Boca Raton: Glove Communications Corp.

Weinstein, A. (2011) TOP 12 MOST FAMOUS ROCKS IN THE UNITED STATES. Article: Listosaur.com. https://listosaur.com/travel/top-12-most-famous-rocks-in-the-united-states/.

Zorrospin, C. (2011) ANCIENT RED-HAIRED GIANTS IN LOVELOCK, NEVADA, USA. Article OTHER WORLD MYSTERY. http://otherworldmystery.com/ancient-red-haired-giants-in-lovelock-nevada-usa.

Christian faith has a new challenge in these modern times, and it seems few are even aware of it. *Angels or Aliens?* provides the knowledge needed to refute these claims and explains where you can find support for your beliefs in the Bible.

Part One: Aliens: The "Alien Mania" currently taking place across the globe, and the effect it is having on the general population is explored. Ongoing scientific findings decreasing the possibility of extraterrestrial life are exposed. Many ancient monoliths that remain across the globe, such as the Great Pyramid and Stonehenge are being used as "proof" that aliens are real and have visited earth. Many of these mysteries are explored here, along with the discoveries of skeletal remains of giants and the increasing reports of UFOs.

Part Two: Angels: Using scripture as foundation, an exploration of these ancient artifacts and who really built them begins. The nature of God and His Laws of Nature, and the fact that God must abide by His own Laws or destroy them is discussed. Using this knowledge, the examination turns to Eric von Daniken, the father of the Ancient Astronaut Theory, and his assertion that God shouldn't need to use a flying vehicle. In the chapters of this section, the First Earth Age spoken of in Second Peter, the truth of Satan's history, the reason for Noah's flood, and the identity of the offspring of the fallen angels are revealed. The reader is then taken on a journey through scripture documenting the incredible technology revealed in the Bible.

Part Three: The Great Deception: An examination of the Parable of the Fig Tree introduced in the thirteenth chapter of Mark begins this section, then the implications of this parable and the possibility we may be close to the "midnight hour" of the last generation are explored. The falling away is documented from Second Thessalonians, which will ultimately create the possibility for the elect to commit the unforgivable sin of the Book of Hebrews. Next, a discerning look at Modern Babylon of today, and how it is affecting our everyday lives. The Book of Amos's hidden dynasties are revealed, along with how they will create and propagate the deception of the end times, that will ultimately usher in the final deception of Satan.

Part Four: The Alien Invasion is a novelette based on scripture and the idea that the Great Deception might involve Satan's return to earth cloaked in the lie that he is an ultra-advanced extraterrestrial from another galaxy. The main protagonists are made up of free-thinking Christians of different denominations that are confronted with Satan's lies and the New Religion he creates. Some of our heroes are common working people, and some are influential members of the clergy. One of the heroes is the President of the United States, and all are spiritually encouraged by the preaching of two old teachers of scripture that strategically appear in Israel.

The story builds to the point where the antagonist, losing support of the world's most powerful, begins to show his super-natural powers attempting to keep the world's nations at bay. Three of our protagonists unite with the two holy men and end time prophesies begin to be fulfilled.

Postscript: Three important End Times ideas are presented, and supported by scripture.

About the Author

The author, Jim Brouillette, is a long-time businessman, college professor and administrator, minister, and Bible student and teacher. Brouillette grew up in Southern California and earned his master's degree in Speech Communication from California State University Long Beach in May of 1977. He began his teaching career in California and continued it after moving to Arizona, where he also became the director of College Services for Arizona Western College in La Paz County. After moving to Arizona, Brouillette was also owner/operator of several small businesses along the Colorado River through the eighties and nineties. After retiring from Arizona Western College, he became the Academic Director of Keiser University's International Language Institute in Managua, Nicaragua for two years, and then taught five semesters at Keiser University's campus in San Marcos, Nicaragua. Now retired from Higher Education, Brouillette lives in Parker Arizona where he enjoys being a father, grandfather, and now great-grandfather. He also continues to write concerning what he believes are the important issues facing modern-day Christians everywhere.